UNPACKING
THE MYSTERIES
OF THE ROSARY

All Bible quotations use the RSVCE unless otherwise noted.

Cover design: Devin Schadt
Formatting: Irena Kalcheva
Copy Proofing: Leisel McBeth & Chris Dipert

Stewardship: Mission of Faith
11 Blackhawk Lane
Elizabethtown, PA 17022
StewardshipMission.org

UNPACKING THE MYSTERIES OF THE ROSARY

Connecting the *Spiritual Fruits* to Your Daily Life

Keith Nester

Edited by
Bud Macfarlane
Xavier A. Macfarlane

FOREWORD

I'm so excited for you! There has never been a book about the Rosary like this one. I know it will surprise you, because it surprised me. I know you will be delighted, because it delighted me. I know this book will change your life, because it changed mine.

A little while back, I heard a guy named Keith Nester tell his amazing story on a podcast. It seemed odd to me at the time, but I remember thinking that we had *the same heart* for souls. Several months later, after a series of "God-incidences," I met him at a conference. He's a short, intense preacher. I'm a big, easy-going writer. Even though we had very different life journeys, we hit it off instantly. Brothers in Christ. Sons of Mary.

Although I'm probably best-known as a novelist, when Keith told me he was planning to write a *very* different kind of Rosary book, I offered to help him with the editing. After he finished the rough draft, he drove from Iowa to our Mary Foundation offices in Ohio to get started. My brilliant son, Xavier, got excited about the ideas when he overheard us working and jumped right in.

That kicked us into overdrive! We worked late into the night as Keith took us "inside" each of the mysteries. There was a surprise within each one, like finding nuggets of gold in your backyard creek.

Everything that follows works so well because it is based on Keith's decades of serving real people as a pastor, the teachings of the Church, the Holy Scriptures, his unique theological insight as a Catholic convert, and especially because Our Lady decided to take him beyond "just saying the words" when he prays the Rosary.

My son and I weren't expecting this book to have such a profound impact on *how we pray and how we live* as followers of Christ, but that's exactly what happened. That's why we're both so excited about what is going to happen in your life when you turn the page.

Bud Macfarlane
President
The Mary Foundation
Feast of the Most Precious Blood of Our Lord Jesus Christ
July 3, 2022

DEDICATION

On March 17, 2020, I did an unscheduled livestream to find out how people were handling the unprecedented Coronavirus events that were rocking the entire globe. Cities were shutting down. People were frightened, angry, and anxious. I just wanted to encourage people. I didn't know if anyone would even join me.

At first, it was just me, and then a few others logged on. The word must've gotten out because soon lots of people started commenting to encourage one another and share what was happening in their towns. It was comforting to feel a sense of community, even with anonymous strangers on YouTube. Someone suggested praying the Rosary together on my channel the following day. Others said they would appreciate this kind of group prayer, so I agreed. We set a time, and I was excited, but I was a little out of my element.

I had been asked to lead the Rosary before, but I always declined. I had been a Catholic for less than three years, so I was still becoming familiar with it. I felt completely unqualified because I was terrified I would make mistakes, talk too fast, or skip something important. However, these were unusual times and I wanted to help. So I mustered up the courage to figure it out.

I found a website called RosaryCenter.org, run by a group of Dominican priests. The website laid out the prayers clearly, which made it easy for me to use as a guide. In addition to listing the mysteries, there was something called a "spiritual fruit" for each mystery. This tradition was new to me. It's a way of diving deeper into each mystery and connecting it to your daily life. I love that sort of thing, so I decided to include them.

The next day we prayed our first Rosary. I did my best, but I made mistakes. The people in the group were very patient and lovingly corrected me. Over time we found our groove. Eventually, I began to share a few of my own thoughts as a way to help us all enter into a deeper level of interaction with the mysteries and spiritual fruits.

Before we knew it, there were hundreds—then thousands—of people from all over the world joining us live or praying with the replay. My wife, Estelle, often sat next to me (off-camera) to welcome people into the chat while I tried my best to stay on top of the tech stuff. People began to connect with each other in deeper ways by sharing their personal intentions and needs. We shared our lives and our love for our faith, Our Lord, and Our Blessed Mother. We were becoming more than a prayer group; we were becoming a family. We named ourselves The Rosary Crew.

To the members of the Rosary Crew:
This book would not exist without you. You will never know how much you have changed our lives. Thank you for your endless love and support. Even though I am the leader of the

Rosary Crew, you have led Estelle and me in so many ways. You encourage and inspire us every day. I hope this book does the same for you. When we get to heaven, let's meet at Mom's house for prayer. Can't wait to see you there.

Keith and Estelle Nester
July 3, 2022

Table of Contents

INTRODUCTION

Not long ago, when I first converted to Catholicism, I was bright-eyed and ready to jump in after spending twenty-two years in full-time ministry as a Protestant. My wife and I were doing the basics by going to Mass and receiving the sacraments. Even so, we wanted much more. I wanted to tap into the profound devotional practices I saw so many Catholics enjoying. The good thing about Catholicism is there is a seemingly unlimited choice of devotions and practices. The tricky thing about Catholicism is there is a seemingly unlimited choice of devotions and practices.

In my first book, *The Convert's Guide to Roman Catholicism: Your First Year in the Church*, I wrote about the need to be realistic when deciding which devotions to choose as a new Catholic. New converts risk burnout and discouragement if they try to do everything all at once. I recommended beginning with the daily Rosary. The Rosary had become an incredible treasure for me almost immediately as I made my way into the

Catholic Church, and I believe it can be a game-changer if you want to supercharge your prayer life.

As with so many other things, *how* we pray the Rosary matters. I am not referring to fast or slow "how-tos" or whether to sit, kneel, or walk during prayer. I am referring to our interior dispositions. In other words, what is happening in our hearts and minds when we pray the Rosary? Are we mindlessly rattling off the words to get through it as quickly as possible? Are we giving the slightest thought to the meaning of the prayers? Or to the mysteries themselves?

When I was a kid, my drum teacher often reminded me, "Practice doesn't make perfect. *Perfect* practice makes perfect." That lesson applies to many things, especially the Rosary. How we pray the Rosary matters. The purpose of this book is to help you understand what it means to encounter the mysteries of the Rosary, and to allow those mysteries to help you practice your prayer perfectly.

Why the Mysteries Matter

What are these mysteries? The word *mystery* itself is confusing because, in common terms, it is defined "as something which is not understood." I tell people that the Mysteries of the Rosary are simply events in the lives of Jesus and His mother provided to help guide our prayers. These mysteries are not random. They are organized into four sets of five. The Joyful Mysteries contain events relating to the conception, birth, and childhood of Jesus through His mother's experience. The Luminous Mysteries reveal the truth about who Jesus is and how He relates to us. The Sorrowful Mysteries detail Our Lord's Passion and take us on a journey to the Cross. The Glorious Mysteries focus on the triumph of Jesus, Mary, and the beginning work of the Church after His Resurrection and Ascension.

During the Rosary, we meditate on each mystery as we pray the ten "Hail Marys" (which is called a "decade"). For some, the term *meditation* is problematic because of its association with eastern religions or new-age practices, which all Catholics should strenuously avoid. However, all Christians have practiced meditative prayer since the time of Christ.

In its basic sense, meditating on the mysteries means focusing intensely on these events and how they can help us grow in holiness. In light of this goal, each mystery has a "spiritual fruit." The spiritual fruit represents a specific virtue associated with each particular mystery. The spiritual fruits have helped me pursue holiness, purity, and perseverance, because I repeatedly "observed" how Jesus and Mary demonstrated these virtues within the actual events of the mysteries.

This realization is huge. Prayer is not about changing God (that's impossible). It's about changing *us*. By digging deeper into the meaning of the mysteries and their spiritual fruits, we will change. A better way to say this: God will change us.

So if you're ready, let's get digging!

Part One

THE JOYFUL MYSTERIES

Rejoice in the Lord always; again I will say rejoice
-St. Paul (Philippians 4:4)

W hen the angels appeared to the shepherds to announce the coming of Jesus, they said, "Be not afraid; for behold, I bring you good news of a great joy which will come to all the people." (Luke 2:10) The events surrounding the birth of Jesus and his early life are the focus of the Joyful Mysteries, for there has never been a better reason to have joy. Jesus has come!

Our joy is rooted not in our current situation but rather in unchangeable historical events. When we look at our everyday circumstances, we can find many reasons not to rejoice. Financial, relational, medical, and other issues can cause us to realize that life stinks. Too often, we think that it's only when our situation changes that we can have joy. Perhaps, the reason for this is we confuse "joy" with "happiness." Happiness is about our emotions, which are significantly impacted by our current situations.

Joy is different. Joy is about the inner state of our soul. It exists on another level of human experience; it does not depend on how we feel on the surface. It doesn't begin with what's going on around us. Joy starts with our relationship with God, knowing God is good and that He loves us. St. Paul wrote while he was in prison, "Rejoice in the Lord always, again I say rejoice." He wasn't focusing on his present situation. He was looking at Christ. The key to joy is just that—keeping our eyes on Jesus.

The Joyful Mysteries take us on a journey primarily from the perspective of the Blessed Mother. Her life was not one of worldly privilege, but as we will see, she has indescribable joy. Her joy can become ours through the Joyful Mysteries.

THE ANNUNCIATION
Spiritual Fruit—Humility

This mystery played a massive role in my conversion to Catholicism. When I was considering the claims of the Catholic Church, I wasn't sure how to process the centrality of the Virgin Mary in Catholicism—most Protestants don't think much about Mary. Typically, sermons about Mary are limited to December because the birth of Jesus is usually a big deal no matter which church you attend.

Leading into Christmas 2016, I was preparing to deliver a series of sermons entitled *Who Gets the News?* These would focus on the moment certain people learned the news about Jesus coming into the world. I preached about the shepherds, St. Joseph, King Herod, Zechariah, and (you guessed it) Mary.

I loved preparing and delivering sermons. During the first week, I spoke about Zechariah, the father of John the Baptist. As I began working on the message for the second week of the series, I opened the Bible to Luke's Gospel. In the Catholic world, verses 26-38 of Chapter 1 portray "The Annunciation." (I didn't call it that back then, it was simply "Luke 1:26-38.") The gospel writer describes the angel Gabriel giving the news about Jesus to a young virgin named Mary:

> *In the sixth month the angel Gabriel was sent from God to a city of Galilee named Nazareth, to a virgin betrothed to a man whose name was Joseph, of the house of David; and the virgin's name was Mary. And he came to her and said, "Hail, full of grace, the Lord is with you!" But she was greatly troubled at the saying, and considered in her mind what sort of greeting this might be. And the angel said to her, "Do not be afraid, Mary, for you have found favor with God. And behold, you will conceive in your womb and bear a son, and you shall call his name Jesus. He will be great, and will be called the Son of the Most High; and the Lord God will give to him the throne of his father David, and he will reign over the house of Jacob forever; and of his kingdom there will be no end." And Mary said to the angel, "How can this be, since I have no husband?" And the angel said to her, "The Holy Spirit will come upon you, and the power of the Most High will overshadow you; therefore the child to be born will be called holy, the Son of God. And behold, your kinswoman Elizabeth in her old age has also conceived a son; and this is the sixth month with her who was called barren. For with God nothing will be impossible." And Mary said, "Behold,*

> *I am the handmaid of the Lord; let it be to me according to*
> *your word." And the angel departed from her.*
>
> (Luke 1:26-38)

As I began to work on the sermon, something started happening. First, new details in the text leaped off the pages. I noticed a stark difference in how Gabriel addressed Zechariah compared to how he initially interacted with Mary. With Zechariah, the angel immediately launched into the message without a formal greeting. This struck me because Zechariah was a priest, but not just a priest. He was righteous and lived blamelessly, according to the text.

Gabriel told him that his wife, Elizabeth, would give birth to a son who would "...turn many of the sons of Israel to the Lord their God, and he will go before him in the spirit and power of Eli'jah, to turn the hearts of the fathers to the children, and the disobedient to the wisdom of the just, to make ready for the Lord a people prepared" (Luke 1:16-17)

But Zechariah did not believe Gabriel! He and Elizabeth had prayed for years for a child, and it hadn't happened. Gabriel's response becomes vital to our understanding of the Mystery of the Annunciation. Zechariah is then told exactly who God has sent to speak to him:

"I am Gabriel, who stand in the presence of God; and I was sent to speak to you, and to bring you this good news." (Luke 1:19) Because of Zechariah's unbelief, Gabriel renders him unable to speak until the child is born.

I mention this because I noticed something profound when I studied how Gabriel greets Mary. The Greek word for the title he gives her, "full of grace," is *Kecharitomene,* which means "completely, perfectly, enduringly endowed with grace." This is quite the greeting for an unassuming, young Jewish girl. As I thought about this, I was overwhelmed with emotion. I had never experienced anything like it before. As I continued preparing the sermon, I got choked up whenever I thought about Mary. (And I rarely get choked up, especially not while preparing sermons.)

There was more to Mary than I realized, and this greeting from Gabriel proved it. What on earth was happening to me? I still can't adequately describe it, but it felt like she was *in the room* with me. A few weeks later, when I told a Catholic friend about my eye-opening experience—*he* started crying. What happened when I prepared that sermon set off a chain of events that drew me into the Catholic Church.

As Mary received the news that she was to conceive and bear a son, she didn't understand how this was possible because she had no relations with a man. Many Catholic scholars and Church Fathers teach that her virginity came from a lifetime vow when she was younger. This explains the tense of the phrase "for I know not man" or "I have no husband." (Luke 1:34)

This tense implies there would be no future change to her virginal state even though she was betrothed to Joseph. Gabriel recognized that Mary's question was different from Zechariah's disbelief. She isn't challenging Gabriel. She just doesn't yet understand how she could become pregnant without the participation of a man. When Gabriel explains to her that the Holy Spirit will overshadow her and she will conceive by the power of God, her response to this incredible message is humble submission, but it goes beyond a simple "yes."

Mary doesn't merely say, "Let it be to me according to thy word." Notice how she says first, "Behold, I am the handmaid of the Lord." Her response relates to her identity. She obeys because of who she is. We can never overstate how important identity is when it comes to our obedience to God. We don't obey because what God says makes sense. We obey because we are His. Mary's response shows that she belongs to God. It doesn't matter if what God asks of her makes sense at the moment. Because she is the handmaid of the Lord, she joyfully accepts.

The spiritual fruit of this mystery is Humility. How can meditating on this mystery foster humility? Let's examine this from two perspectives.

It's easy to see the humility of Mary. She submits her life to the will of God in a way that will change everything. It may be hard to imagine, but Mary never planned to be a mother! Mary didn't understand how all this would work, but she obeyed. This type of obedience takes humility. When God reveals His plans for us, we must set aside our plans. We must humble ourselves before whatever God asks of us. "Let it be to me according to the Thy word," Mary says. Can we do that?

For many of us, when the Word of God comes, we want to know everything first, *before* we agree. We want to ensure we are okay with the costs of following God's will. We want to make sure that God's plan matches up with our plan. It's human nature.

Unfortunately, when we set these types of preconditions to our obedience, we fail to *live into* what God has for us. This is why humility is so necessary. Humility removes the boundaries around our submission. Unconditional obedience is where joy begins! Joy comes from humbly receiving Jesus in a way that is ultimate and complete. When we refuse to obey God because of the costs involved or because His will doesn't align with our plans, we cut ourselves off from more joy than we can imagine. Mary's joy is limitless, not only because of her love for God, but also due to her willingness to step into whatever God asks.

The second perspective to examine is Gabriel's. He is one of the most powerful beings ever created and stands in the presence of God Almighty. Yet when he approaches Mary, he does so humbly. He doesn't say to her, "I'm a big deal—do what I say or else." He recognizes her as "highly favored" or "full of grace." I bet for Gabriel this was an honor. Of all the angels, *he was chosen* to announce this good news to the Mother of God. Perhaps another angel would have been less excited about greeting a mere human in this way. Gabriel's humility before Mary proves that he was the best choice for such an incredible mission.

How does Gabriel's humility inspire you? Sometimes we can fall into the trap of believing we deserve better than what God asks of us. Have you ever felt like some tasks were beneath you? Have you ever heard a call for volunteers and thought,

I'm not doing that because it was something that didn't excite you? This can happen to all of us. Whether we like to admit it or not, sometimes our pride keeps us from receiving incredible blessings.

One of the most influential persons in my spiritual growth was a man who ran a summer camp for young people. His name was Stan. He was the least outdoorsy person you could imagine. God had called him to start a small camp where a few kids could hear the gospel and dedicate their lives to Jesus. Stan hated to be uncomfortable and had no desire to be in the woods with a bunch of screaming kids and bugs, but his faithfulness was stronger than his preferences. His small camp became a movement of God where *thousands* of young people would find their faith, including me.

Here is the lesson from Gabriel: accept whatever assignment God brings to you. Don't let pride keep you from being used in whatever way God chooses. Remember, whatever God calls you to, is the best possible thing you can do.

What have you heard from God but rejected because it didn't make sense to you? Remember, we have two choices. We can be like Zechariah and, out of pride, refuse to believe, or we can imitate the humility of this young woman named Mary and receive more joy than we could ever imagine. What haven't you accepted? Be like Gabriel, and with humility, step up. To be who God wants us to be and do what He wants us to do, we *must* be humble.

This is what the Annunciation is all about.

THE VISITATION
Spiritual Fruit—Love of Neighbor

When people want to understand where to find the prayers of the Rosary in the Bible, the Second Joyful Mystery is essential. People often ask me, "Where is the Rosary in the Bible?" I understand why. Something crucial to a person's faith should be grounded in scripture. So, what's the answer? Here's how I respond: the Rosary was developed nearly a thousand years after the Ascension of Jesus. Why would anyone expect (or even claim) that the Bible would mention it by name? No Catholic says, "Pray the Rosary because the Bible says so."

The development of devotions over the centuries is part of what makes the Catholic Church awesome. Holy men and women have created numerous ways to help people grow more devoted to Christ. To insist that the Bible must mention every devotional practice explicitly is not only unrealistic but self-contradicting. Where does the Bible say every devotion must be found in the Bible? Not to mention, the Bible itself doesn't tell us which books belong in the Bible. So when people challenge me with "Where is the Rosary in the Bible?" I sometimes answer, "Where is the *Bible* in the Bible?" People usually make a strange face or tell me I'm crazy. I may be crazy, but I never get a good answer.

There is a crucial distinction between something being found *in the contents* of the Bible and something being developed *from the contents* of the Bible. We won't find a verse that says "Pray the Rosary," but that in no way makes the Rosary unbiblical.

Here's how Luke describes the Visitation between Mary and Elizabeth (Zechariah's wife):

> *In those days Mary arose and went with haste into the hill country, to a city of Judah, and she entered the house of Zechariah and greeted Elizabeth. And when Elizabeth heard the greeting of Mary, the babe leaped in her womb; and Elizabeth was filled with the Holy Spirit and she exclaimed with a loud cry, "Blessed are you among women, and blessed is the fruit of your womb! And why is this granted me, that the mother of my Lord should come to me? For behold, when the voice of your greeting came to my ears, the babe in my womb leaped for joy. And blessed is she who believed that there would be a fulfillment of what was spoken to her from the Lord." And Mary said,*
>
> *"My soul magnifies the Lord, and my spirit rejoices in God my Savior, for he has regarded the low estate of his handmaiden.*

*For behold, henceforth all generations will call me blessed;
for he who is mighty has done great things for me, and holy
is his name. And his mercy is on those who fear him from
generation to generation. He has shown strength with his
arm, he has scattered the proud in the imagination of their
hearts, he has put down the mighty from their thrones, and
exalted those of low degree; he has filled the hungry with
good things, and the rich he has sent empty away. He has
helped his servant Israel, in remembrance of his mercy, as
he spoke to our fathers, to Abraham and to his posterity for
ever." And Mary remained with her about three months, and
returned to her home.*

(Luke 1:39-56)

Did you see it? The "Hail Mary" prayer is taken word-for-word
from Gabriel and Elizabeth's greetings. I love how Luke tells us
that Elizabeth was filled with the Holy Spirit when she cries
out, "Blessed are you among women, and blessed is the fruit
of your womb." Elizabeth then identifies Mary as the "mother
of my Lord." These verses speak for themselves. As we journey
through the mysteries, we will learn more about the rest of
the Hail Mary, "Pray for us sinners, now and at the hour of our
death." For now, let's focus on The Visitation.

Luke's account of Mary's journey to visit Elizabeth is about
much more than a family reunion. He highlights this event to
demonstrate some significant theological truths about Mary,
specifically her role as the "New Ark of the Covenant" and the

"Mother of God." A casual reading of the text shows us Elizabeth's statement that Mary is "the mother of my Lord." To understand the fullness of what Luke is saying, we must read his writing next to the Old Testament writings of the prophet Samuel. In 2nd Samuel, chapter 6, the prophet describes another visitation, the Ark of the Covenant traveling to Jerusalem. See if you can spot the similarities:

> *"How can the ark of the Lord come to me?"*   (2 Samuel 6:9)

> *"And why is this granted me, that the mother of my Lord should come to me?"*   (Luke 1:43)

> *"And David danced before the Lord with all his might."*   (2 Samuel 6:14)

> *"And when Elizabeth heard the greeting of Mary, the babe leaped in her womb."*   (Luke 1:41)

> *"And the ark of the Lord remained in the house of O'bed-e'dom the Gittite three months."*   (2 Samuel 6:11)

> *"And Mary remained with her about three months, and returned to her home."*   (Luke 1:56)

There are certainly more similarities, but Luke ensures we see that Mary is the New Ark of the Covenant. Like the Ark, she contains the physical presence of God on earth. Many Church Fathers saw this parallel. For example, St. Ambrose taught,

> *The prophet David danced before the Ark. Now what else should we say the Ark was but holy Mary? The Ark bore within it the tables of the Testament, but Mary bore the Heir of the same Testament itself. The former contained in it the Law, the latter the Gospel. The one had the voice of God, the other His Word. The Ark, indeed, was radiant within and without with the glitter of gold, but holy Mary shone within and without with the splendor of virginity. The one was adorned with earthly gold, the other with heavenly.*
>
> (Serm. xlii. 6, Int. Opp., S. Ambrosii. Fourth Century)

Many more Church Fathers confirm what Luke showed us in the Bible. Understanding Mary's role as the "mother of my Lord," and as the New Ark of the Covenant, is part of what makes the Rosary so incredible. When we meditate on this mystery, Mary comes to us in our own "visitation." Like Elizabeth, we can be filled with the Holy Spirit. Like the baby in Elizabeth's womb, we can leap for joy every time we pray the Rosary (at least on the inside).

A *joyful* mystery indeed!

The spiritual fruit of this mystery is Love of Neighbor. St. Paul instructs us to "Rejoice with those who rejoice, weep with those who weep." (Romans 12:15). We often tend to focus on the "weep with those who weep" part because of the practical desire to show compassion when we see someone suffering. As important as it is to help others carry their crosses, loving our neighbor also requires celebrating the blessings God brings into our lives. The fullness of our relationships must include both.

When we truly love one another, we celebrate other people's blessings more than our own. This is exactly what we see in The Visitation. Mary traveled approximately eighty miles to rejoice in God's blessing in the life of her cousin Elizabeth. That's commitment. Mary was motivated by a desire to help her pregnant cousin—and also to celebrate. When she arrives, Elizabeth's joy is through the roof, and so is Mary's. These two women of God and their unborn sons share a glimpse of heaven. They worship God together and give thanks for His goodness in their lives.

Friends, we need to do more of this. We are inclined to spring into action when we see a person in crisis, but do we have the same urgency when it comes to rejoicing with others? We may "like" a post online or send a card when we see something good happening in the life of a friend, but these minimal acknowledgments aren't enough to truly "rejoice with those who rejoice." It seems like we'd want to do more, but something holds us back.

Why is celebrating the good such a struggle? Sometimes we're our own worst enemy. When we see good things happening to others, we can wonder, *why don't good things happen to me?* Then we feel horrible for being jealous or envious, but the reaction is there. Then, assuming other people might react the way we do, we downplay or hide our blessings because we don't want to make others feel bad about the good things in our lives. This motivates us to avoid "bragging," but cuts us off from rejoicing together. The entire dynamic is frustrating, isn't it?

Because joy multiplies when you share it with others, the evil one will keep us in these psychological mazes to make sure we don't rejoice together. Sharing our joy, like Mary and Elizabeth did, is the way out. This is why Love of Neighbor is the spiritual fruit of this mystery.

As we meditate on The Visitation, let us ask Our Lord to help us *genuinely* desire good in the lives of others, so that motivated by that desire, we can rejoice with them and unlock tremendous joy.

THE NATIVITY
Spiritual Fruit—Detachment

*Joy to the world, the Lord is come. Let earth receive
her King. Let every heart prepare him room.*
-Issac Watts

The birth of Jesus changed everything. For centuries people looked toward the coming Messiah, The Anointed One. Roughly seven centuries before Jesus was born, the prophet Isaiah wrote, "The people who walked in darkness have seen a great light; those who dwelt in a land of deep darkness, on them has light shined." (Isaiah 9:2)

The Old Testament prophets foretold of a great king who would rule the world. Isaiah continues, "Of the increase of his government and of peace there will be no end, upon the throne of David, and over his kingdom, to establish it, and to uphold it with justice and with righteousness from this time forth and for evermore. The zeal of the Lord of hosts will do this." (Isaiah 9:7)

These verses should look familiar. The angel Gabriel quotes this text in the Annunciation, referring to Jesus. (How cool would it be to be quoted by an angel?) It's easy to understand how people would expect the coming Messiah to be a great king who would liberate the Jews from the Roman occupation. They had a tragic history of exile and defeat at the hands of their enemies. The promise of a king was an encouragement and a hope. What would the circumstances be surrounding his birth? How would he enter the world? The answer is found in the Nativity:

> *In those days a decree went out from Caesar Augustus that all the world should be enrolled. This was the first enrollment, when Quirin'i-us was governor of Syria. And all went to be enrolled, each to his own city. And Joseph also went up from Galilee, from the city of Nazareth, to Judea, to the city of David, which is called Bethlehem, because he was of the house and lineage of David, to be enrolled with Mary, his betrothed, who was with child. And while they were there, the time came for her to be delivered. And she gave birth to her first-born son and wrapped him in swaddling cloths, and laid him in a manger, because there was no place for them in the inn.*
>
> *And in that region there were shepherds out in the field, keeping watch over their flock by night. And an angel of*

the Lord appeared to them, and the glory of the Lord shone around them, and they were filled with fear. And the angel said to them, "Be not afraid; for behold, I bring you good news of a great joy which will come to all the people; for to you is born this day in the city of David a Savior, who is Christ the Lord. And this will be a sign for you: you will find a babe wrapped in swaddling cloths and lying in a manger." And suddenly there was with the angel a multitude of the heavenly host praising God and saying, "Glory to God in the highest, and on earth peace among men with whom he is pleased!"

When the angels went away from them into heaven, the shepherds said to one another, "Let us go over to Bethlehem and see this thing that has happened, which the Lord has made known to us." And they went with haste, and found Mary and Joseph, and the babe lying in a manger. And when they saw it they made known the saying which had been told them concerning this child; and all who heard it wondered at what the shepherds told them. But Mary kept all these things, pondering them in her heart. And the shepherds returned, glorifying and praising God for all they had heard and seen, as it had been told them.

(Luke 2:1-20)

The King had arrived, but His mission was not the expected liberation from the Romans. Jesus came to "save his people from their sins." (Matthew 1:21) Many religious leaders could not grasp this. Jesus did not meet their expectations, so they rejected Him. This trend continues. People want a Jesus who will liberate them from their bad circumstances or their disappointments. Jesus has other plans. He wants to deliver us from sin. He wants to meet our ultimate need—forgiveness.

The Nativity shows us that even in His birth, Jesus was not concerned with worldly acclaim or comfort. His cradle was a feeding trough. His parents were poor. But don't think for one minute that there wasn't joy when Jesus was born. The angels rejoiced! The shepherds came and praised God. Mary kept all these things, pondering them in her heart. Mary knew that the miraculous birth of her Son would forever change the world. She was full of joy.

Real joy comes from knowing Jesus' true purpose, because His mission is more significant than we can imagine. Too often, we seek God for the mundane. A good job. Physical health. Material needs. These things are fine, but Jesus has come to give us so much more. He has come to reconcile us to the Father. Forgiveness is our greatest need. In the Nativity, God the Father gives us the greatest gift in His one and only Son. To receive this gift, we must have open arms.

The spiritual fruit of this mystery is Detachment. Jesus knows a thing or two about detachment. St. Paul wrote in his letter to the Philippians, "Have this mind among yourselves, which was in Christ Jesus, who, though he was in the form of God, did not count equality with God a thing to be grasped, but emptied himself, taking the form of a servant, being born in the likeness of men." (Phil 2:5-7)

Think about everything Jesus detached from to be with us on earth. He became a humble servant born into a dark world. He wasn't born into affluence, comfort, or an easy life. Even if He were, it would have been nothing compared to what He left behind in heaven. Jesus detached from heaven and came to earth, so we could detach from earth and go to heaven.

Detachment makes saints. When we look at their lives, we see their ability to step into a level of holiness and joy that amazes us. Consider St. Maximilian Kolbe, who detached himself from the expectation of living so he could save another person's life. Consider St. Faustina, who detached herself from the acceptance of her peers so she could be an apostle of mercy who changed the world. There are countless more examples of men and women who have allowed God to do great things in their lives. The common thread they share is detachment. The spiritual fruit of Detachment is saying to God, "I am ready to receive all you want to give."

When I was wrestling with quitting my job in ministry to become Catholic, I saw a cartoon image online of a little girl holding a teddy bear with both hands. She was facing Jesus, who was holding an enormous teddy bear hidden behind His back with one hand, while reaching out to her with His other hand, asking to take the much smaller bear.

"But I love it," she said, clutching the small bear.

"Trust Me," said Jesus.

Jesus' bear was so big that the child would need both hands to hold it. Because she couldn't see the bigger bear, she didn't want to let go of the smaller one. This is a picture of the human condition. Too often, we are holding on for dear life to the things we think we need. Jesus stands before us with so much more to give. To make room for God's blessings, we must clear out whatever is taking up space. This is the essence of "detachment." We must let go of anything that would keep us from Jesus' mission to forgive our sins.

Detachment is tough stuff. When God tries to bless you in unexpected ways, you realize how much you are holding onto. What are you so attached to? What would you refuse to give up, even if Jesus asked for it? Remember, Jesus loves you and wants the best for you. Do you trust Him? Will you let Him take care of you? Or do you believe you are better at taking care of yourself? If we want joy, we need to trust Jesus. We need to detach.

God rest ye merry gentlemen, let nothing you dismay.
Remember Christ our Savior was born on Christmas
Day. To save us all from Satan's pow'r, when we were
gone astray, oh tidings of comfort and joy.
-Author Unknown

The Fourth Joyful Mystery

THE PRESENTATION
Spiritual Fruit—Obedience

The Lord said to Moses, "Consecrate to me
all the first-born; whatever is the first to open
the womb among the people of Israel, both
of man and of beast, is mine."

(Exodus 13:1-2)

When my daughter Devon was born, the universe exploded. Okay, I'm being a little dramatic, but that's how it felt. I wanted everyone to see this amazing miracle. It was as if she was the only baby in the world. To me, she was. First-time parents feel that excitement. They believe their baby is the cutest baby ever. They tell everyone, "You have to come see the baby!" I don't think this was any different for Mary and Joseph. Jesus had exploded their universe.

The book of Exodus required firstborn sons to be consecrated to the Lord. This was a big deal for the Hebrews. The parents were to go to the Temple in Jerusalem and redeem back their son, to honor what God did in Egypt when He slew the first-born sons of the Egyptians, leading to the deliverance of the Israelites. Additionally, in the book of Leviticus, the Lord, through Moses, instructed that new mothers must be ritually purified after giving birth. This dual presentation and purification was to take place forty days after the birth of the child.

We must call to mind two important facts:

1. Jesus is the Son of God. He was already consecrated by virtue of His nature.

2. Mary was not made impure by Jesus' birth, so technically, she didn't need ritual purification.

Nevertheless, to observe the Law of Moses, Mary and Joseph fulfilled the requirements. I don't think they would've had it any other way. This wasn't a "have-to." The Presentation was a "get-to." This was a proud moment for Mary and Joseph. Imagine how they felt when they brought their beautiful new baby to the Temple to fulfill their duty to the Law and dedicate their family to the work of God:

And when the time came for their purification according to the law of Moses, they brought him up to Jerusalem to present him to the Lord (as it is written in the law of the Lord, "Every male that opens the womb shall be called holy to the Lord") and to offer a sacrifice according to what is said in the law of the Lord, "a pair of turtledoves, or two young pigeons." Now there was a man in Jerusalem, whose name was Simeon, and this man was righteous and devout, looking for the consolation of Israel, and the Holy Spirit was upon him. And it had been revealed to him by the Holy Spirit that he should not see death before he had seen the Lord's Christ. And inspired by the Spirit he came into the temple; and when the parents brought in the child Jesus, to do for him according to the custom of the law, he took him up in his arms and blessed God and said, "Lord, now lettest thou thy servant depart in peace, according to thy word; for mine eyes have seen thy salvation which thou hast prepared in the presence of all peoples, a light for revelation to the Gentiles, and for glory to thy people Israel."

And his father and his mother marveled at what was said about him; and Simeon blessed them and said to Mary his mother, "Behold, this child is set for the fall and rising of many in Israel, and for a sign that is spoken against (and a sword will pierce through your own soul also), that thoughts out of many hearts may be revealed."

And there was a prophetess, Anna, the daughter of Phanu-el, of the tribe of Asher; she was of a great age, having lived with her husband seven years from her virginity, and as a widow till she was eighty-four. She did not depart from the temple, worshiping with fasting and prayer night and day.

And coming up at that very hour she gave thanks to God, and spoke of him to all who were looking for the redemption of Jerusalem.

And when they had performed everything according to the law of the Lord, they returned into Galilee, to their own city, Nazareth. And the child grew and became strong, filled with wisdom; and the favor of God was upon him.

(Luke 2:22-40)

A lot is going on in this mystery. In addition to the Presentation of Jesus and the Purification of Mary, two key people are mentioned in the text. Simeon and Anna had waited patiently for the Messiah. They weren't there for the Nativity, but God was faithful to them and in the Presentation, God gave them a special role. Simeon's entire life had led him to this moment. He knew he wouldn't die until he had *seen* the promised Messiah, but Simeon actually *held* Jesus in his hands! Imagine the joy.

Mary and Joseph had to feel incredible hearing the words from this holy old man. Yet, even in their joy, there was a realization that God's plan for the child and His parents would require sacrifice and pain. Simeon's chilling words warned Mary that her role as the Mother of God would not be easy. She would bear a burden like no one else.

Anna, the prophetess, had spent much of her life fasting and praying in the Temple. When she saw Jesus, she gave thanks to God, giving her testimony that the Redeemer of Israel was in their midst. Mary and Joseph didn't have worldly possessions or social status, but I would bet my last dollar they had joy overflowing.

Jesus' Presentation to God foreshadows His crucifixion when He would be presented as the Lamb of God who takes away the sins of the world. The Presentation of Jesus continues in every Holy Sacrifice of the Mass when He is *re*-presented. To God, and to us.

The spiritual fruit of this mystery is Obedience. Mary and Joseph obeyed God in everything. So did Simeon and Anna. The result was complete joy. Obedience leads to joy. We are each called to our own *presentation*. St. Paul was clear: "I appeal to you therefore, brethren, by the mercies of God, to present your bodies as a living sacrifice, holy and acceptable to God, which is your spiritual worship." (Romans 12:1)

Every day we wake up is a new chance for a *presentation*. The level of joy we receive is directly related to the level of obedience we present to God. What are you presenting to God?

Are you like Mary and Joseph? Full of wonder and amazement as you bring yourself and everything you have before God? Or, are you lukewarm and make excuses for your partial, half-hearted obedience?

Are you like Simeon, who waited patiently until the Holy Spirit called him to receive the promised blessing of seeing the Messiah? Or, are you too focused on your own desires to respond to the leading of the Holy Spirit?

Are you like Anna, presenting herself daily in worship and thanksgiving? Or, have you become too busy chasing the world to take time to worship God? If you want joy, then stand before God in obedience. Right now. Everything you have. Offer it all to God. That's what the Presentation is all about.

FINDING JESUS IN THE TEMPLE
Spiritual Fruit—Perseverance

When our son Jesse was four years old, my wife Estelle and I lost him in a crowded fairground parking lot. It was a sunny day and thousands of people were milling about. The smell of cotton candy was in the air, and lively music flowed from a band on the stage. Jesse was walking a little bit behind us with a couple we knew. When the husband came up to talk to us, we noticed Jesse wasn't with him.

Estelle asked him, "Where's Jesse?"

"I dunno," he replied.

Estelle and I panicked. There were hundreds of people moving in all directions. We spun around to see if we could find Jesse. There was no sign of him. I have never felt more afraid in my life. We all spread out and shouted his name. We found him at a vendor's booth a few minutes later, calmly looking at some toys. Our relief was immense. All was well in the world again. Losing a child is terrifying. Finding one is an indescribable joy.

In the fifth Joyful Mystery, we experience both feelings (terror and joy) through Mary and Joseph. It's important to remember the focus of this mystery is the joy of finding Jesus, *not* the panic of losing Him. However, you can't have one without the other. Let's take a look:

> *Now his parents went to Jerusalem every year at the feast of the Passover. And when he was twelve years old, they went up according to custom; and when the feast was ended, as they were returning, the boy Jesus stayed behind in Jerusalem. His parents did not know it, but supposing him to be in the company they went a day's journey, and they sought him among their kinsfolk and acquaintances; and when they did not find him, they returned to Jerusalem, seeking him. After three days they found him in the temple, sitting among the teachers, listening to them and asking them questions; and all who heard him were amazed at his understanding and his answers. And when they saw him they were astonished; and his mother said to him, "Son, why have you treated us so? Behold, your father and I have been looking for you anxiously." And he said to them, "How is it that you sought me? Did you not know that I must be in my Father's house?" And they did not understand the saying which he spoke to them. And he went down with them and came to Nazareth, and was obedient to them; and his mother kept all these things in her heart.*

> (Luke 2:41-51)

Imagine how Mary and Joseph felt when they realized Jesus wasn't with them. They had been traveling for an entire day before they figured out He was gone. The panic and terror must have been unimaginable. Remember, they didn't know the end of the story. No one said, "It's okay, this is Luke 2:41-51, you'll find Him in the Temple." They felt the weight of the responsibility to care for the Son of God. Had they failed? Where could He have gone? Did someone take Him?

Note that the moment they realized they weren't with Jesus, they stopped, turned around, and went back to the last place they were with Him. We will all experience moments when we realize we aren't with Jesus. There are so many things that can take us away. Our sin, obviously, but also being lazy in our faith or being afraid to follow Jesus. Remember, Jesus was never lost. Mary and Joseph just left without Him. When they realized this—they simply went back. Going back to Jesus is something we all have to do. The biblical term for this is *repentance*.

The spiritual fruit of this mystery is Perseverance. Mary and Joseph spent three days looking for Jesus. They would have spent the rest of their lives if that's what it took. Perseverance is vital to the life of a disciple. Jesus has called us to follow Him, but there are times when we go the other way, lag behind, or in this case, get ahead of Him. When we realize something isn't right and we aren't with Him, we need to stop and go back. It can feel like Jesus is lost, but in reality, we are the ones who get lost. Jesus never gets lost.

Finding your way back to Him can be difficult. It all depends on how far you have ventured away, but understand this—Jesus is not hiding from you. When Mary and Joseph found Jesus in the Temple, He wasn't anxious. He wasn't afraid or worried. Jesus seems surprised that it took them so long to figure out where He was. "How is it that you sought me? Did you not know that I must be in my Father's house?"

Jesus wasn't hiding from His parents, and He is not hiding from you. He tells them and us exactly where He is—the Father's house. When you need to get back to Jesus, go back to the Father's house. Go back to the Church. Don't quit. Don't let shame or guilt keep you away. Think about how Mary and Joseph must have felt. They were entrusted with caring for the Son of God, and they lost Him! How easy would it have been for them to feel like failures and give up? But they didn't give up. They persevered until they found Him.

We must do the same. We must ignore those voices that tell us we've strayed too far and are irredeemable. Let's examine the story of the Prodigal Son. When he realized he needed to get back to his father, he wasn't miraculously transported home. He had to pick himself up, turn around, and take the first step of the long journey back. He had to persevere.

Along the way, there are so many things he probably wondered. Is this a good idea? Will I be accepted? Will I be allowed back into the presence of my father? When he was within eyesight, the father ran to him joyfully and kissed him.

The Prodigal Son was welcomed home with a feast. The same is true for us. When we make our way back to Jesus, it won't always be easy, but it will always be worth it.

Even though this mystery is about finding Jesus, He also understands a thing or two about perseverance and the joy that comes from finding a lost son or daughter.

> *What man of you, having a hundred sheep, if he has lost one of them, does not leave the ninety-nine in the wilderness, and go after the one which is lost, until he finds it? And when he has found it, he lays it on his shoulders, rejoicing. And when he comes home, he calls together his friends and his neighbors, saying to them, 'Rejoice with me, for I have found my sheep which was lost.' Just so, I tell you, there will be more joy in heaven over one sinner who repents than over ninety-nine righteous persons who need no repentance.*
>
> (Luke 15:4-7)

Part of finding your way back to Jesus is letting Him find you. This is what the Fifth Joyful Mystery is all about.

Closing Thoughts

on The Joyful Mysteries

Never underestimate the power of joy. Joy affects us internally but also spills out into those around us. When people can see our joy, especially in difficult circumstances, they will want to know the source. There are few things more effective in reaching people than the joyful Christian.

Jesus reassures us, "These things I have spoken to you, that my joy may be in you, and that your joy may be full." (John 15:11) We must never forget that joy is God's will for us. The Joyful Mysteries help us to live the Christian life to the fullest, because they connect us to the source of our greatest joy—Jesus. May our hearts cry out in praise, and may our spirits rejoice in God our savior!

Part Two

THE LUMINOUS MYSTERIES

The Mysteries of Light were officially added to the Rosary by Pope St. John Paul II in 2002 in the Apostolic Letter *Rosarium Virginis Mariae*, Paragraph 19:

> *...it would be suitable to make an addition to the traditional pattern which, while left to the freedom of individuals and communities, could broaden it to include the mysteries of Christ's public ministry between his Baptism and his Passion. In the course of those mysteries we contemplate important aspects of the person of Christ as the definitive revelation of God.*

These mysteries are rightly called luminous because they do what light does. They reveal truth—the truth about what is around us. Light doesn't create truth, rather, it simply shows us what is already there. The function of the Luminous Mysteries is the same: they reveal the truth about Jesus.

Light also guides us. Without light, we stumble through life, crashing into things and hurting ourselves. In the same way, the truths in the Luminous Mysteries guide us. Without a proper understanding of Jesus, we stumble through life, crashing into things and hurting ourselves.

Lastly, light comforts us. When I was a child, my parents moved me into a bedroom with no windows. When the door was shut, and the lights were off, it was pitch black. Darkness is helpful when you're trying to sleep, but too much darkness can terrify a kid. So, my mom saved the day by bringing in a nightlight. That nightlight provided just enough light to ease my fear of a giant monster standing over me as I slept.

For adults, when the days grow shorter in winter, our tempers and moods often follow suit. This is because there is less light. Without enough daylight, we can become depressed and gloomy. No one really understands why, but it's true. Light comforts us. In the same way, the truth of Jesus comforts us. Let's unpack the Luminous Mysteries to find out how to live our fullest lives in the light of His glory.

THE BAPTISM OF JESUS
Spiritual Fruit—Openness to the Holy Spirit

The most important truth in the universe is that Jesus is the Son of God. If He is God, then everything He says and does is true. In the Baptism of Jesus, we see (and hear) the truth about Jesus. Just as light reveals reality, the Baptism of Jesus reveals His true identity.

Jesus and John had known each other even before they were born. In the second Joyful Mystery, we saw John the Baptist leap for joy inside the womb of his mother Elizabeth when he encountered Jesus in the womb of Mary. One can only imagine the dynamic with these two running around during family get-togethers. Not much is known about their childhood relationship, but since they were almost the same age and their mothers were cousins, it's likely they were close.

As they grew up, each developed his own ministry. John the Baptist's came first as he retreated into the wilderness to live a life of separation from the world. He preached fiery sermons and called even the religious leaders to repentance. Many followed his teachings and demonstrated their repentance and devotion to God by being baptized in the Jordan River.

His baptism of repentance is distinguished from the baptism that would soon become the principal sacrament of the Christian faith. John's own revelation is striking: "I baptize you with water for repentance, but he who is coming after me is mightier than I, whose sandals I am not worthy to carry; he will baptize you with the Holy Spirit and with fire." (Matthew 3:11)

Furthermore, John also gives us incredible insights into the identity of Jesus. "The next day, he saw Jesus coming toward him and said, 'Behold, the Lamb of God, who takes away the sin of the world!'" (John 1:29) This statement is the key moment in the Luminous Mysteries. John explicitly connects Jesus to the ancient promise in Genesis when Abraham said to Isaac, "God himself will provide the lamb for the burnt offering, my son." (Genesis 22:8) The *Lamb of God* is a principal identity statement about Jesus; it reveals His *mission*. Everything we will see in the Luminous Mysteries flows from this truth:

> *Then Jesus came from Galilee to the Jordan to John, to be baptized by him. John would have prevented him, saying, "I need to be baptized by you, and do you come to me?" But Jesus answered him, "Let it be so now; for thus it is fitting for us to fulfill all righteousness." Then he consented. And when Jesus was baptized, he went up immediately from the water, and behold, the heavens were opened and he saw the Spirit*

> *of God descending like a dove, and alighting on him; and lo,*
> *a voice from heaven, saying, "This is my beloved Son, with*
> *whom I am well pleased."*
>
> (Matthew 3:13-17)

Even though John was more well-known at that time, when Jesus presented Himself for baptism, John resisted because he recognized the supremacy of Jesus. Jesus then directed John and was baptized. Let's explore this.

John's question about the need for Jesus' baptism was reasonable. After all, Jesus had never sinned, so the baptism of repentance wasn't needed. So why was Jesus baptized? The answer is found in Jesus' words above. "It is fitting for us to fulfill all righteousness."

I don't pretend to understand all that Jesus means by this statement. But I am sure of one thing: John's doubts about his worthiness to baptize Jesus belonged only to John, not Jesus. Baptism is about more than just repentance. It's about God's provision and covenant promise. In baptism, we are set apart as the people of God. The early Christians saw the connection between the sign of the Old Covenant (circumcision) and the sign of the New Covenant (baptism). Jesus tells Nicodemus that without baptism, a person cannot even see the kingdom of God. (John 3:3) It's fitting then, that Jesus, the King, would also be baptized.

Baptism initiates us into the family of God. Through baptism, we are "born again." We are given a new identity in Christ. For Jesus, baptism was also a revelation of another element of His identity. The voice from heaven declares, "This is my beloved Son." The first mystery of light reveals the most important truth in the universe: Jesus is the Son of the Father. The triune nature of God is also revealed when the Spirit of God descends on Jesus like a dove. So much truth. So much reality. So much for us to learn.

The spiritual fruit of this mystery is Openness to the Holy Spirit. I like to think of this fruit from the perspective of John the Baptist because I can relate to his feelings of unworthiness. God often calls us to things we don't think we can or should do. I have felt this many times in my life. When I first entered into youth ministry, I was barely twenty years old, a college dropout, and had zero experience. The church that hired me saw something in me I certainly didn't see in myself.

During the interview with the hiring committee, one of the women asked how I would handle a student confiding in me something that could be dangerous. "I have no clue how I would deal with that," I answered. I was convinced I was utterly unqualified for the job and remember praying that night, "God, if you want me to do this, I will. But I am sure you don't." Two days later, they offered me the job. I spent thirteen years in that position and experienced incredible ministry.

Being open to the Holy Spirit means allowing God to run your life without your objections standing in the way. It's human to question things. Many saints have felt unworthy and wondered if God was making a mistake by calling them into their vocation, but what separates those who see God work powerfully in their lives from those who don't, is obedience. Like the Blessed Virgin Mary, who didn't understand how Gabriel's words to her could come to pass—"*How can this be since I know not man?*"—John the Baptist didn't know how he could be worthy of baptizing Jesus. He did it anyway. *That's* openness to the Holy Spirit.

Meditating on this mystery shows us two things: that Jesus is the Son of God, and that we must pay more attention to what *He says* about us than what *we say* about ourselves. As disciples of Jesus, we must embrace the reality that God will call us to things we could never do without Him. That's the essence of a life of openness to the Holy Spirit. That's the truth of this first Luminous Mystery.

THE WEDDING AT CANA
Spiritual Fruit—To Jesus Through Mary

Wedding feasts are a big deal in the Bible. That's because marriage is a big deal in the Bible. Marriage is a sacrament because it is both a means of grace and a divinely instituted image of the relationship between Jesus and the Church. St. Paul explains it this way: "'For this reason, a man shall leave his father and mother and be joined to his wife, and the two shall become one flesh.' This is a great mystery, and I mean in reference to Christ and the church." (Ephesians 5:31-32)

Jesus used the imagery of a wedding banquet in a parable describing what it's like to be invited into the Kingdom of Heaven. A king was planning a great banquet for his son's wedding. Invitations were sent out and everything was prepared, but the invited guests refused. The king wanted a full house, so he instructed his servants to invite people off the street and bring in anyone who would respond. (Matthew 22:1-14)

Jesus was teaching that God had invited His chosen people, the Jews, to celebrate His Son's union with His people, but they had refused. So God extended His invitation to others, the Gentiles. There is more to unpack in this parable, but the point is that the *wedding* imagery is no accident. Weddings are a big deal in the Bible.

In Revelation, St. John describes another wedding banquet. This one is in heaven and is called the Marriage Supper of the Lamb:

> *Then I heard what seemed to be the voice of a great multitude, like the sound of many waters and like the sound of mighty thunderpeals, crying,*
>
> *"Hallelujah! For the Lord our God the Almighty reigns.*
>
> *Let us rejoice and exult and give him the glory,*
>
> *for the marriage of the Lamb has come, and his Bride has made herself ready;*
>
> *it was granted her to be clothed with fine linen, bright and pure"—*
>
> *for the fine linen is the righteous deeds of the saints. And the angel said to me, "Write this: Blessed are those who are invited to the marriage supper of the Lamb." And he said to me, These are true words of God."*
>
> (Revelation 19:6-9)

Understanding the importance of this imagery helps us dive deeply into the second Luminous Mystery. We know from John's Gospel that there were vastly more things he could've written about Jesus. John carefully selected his material under the inspiration of the Holy Spirit. There is nothing arbitrary here. What comes next is profound. Illuminating.

> *On the third day there was a marriage at Cana in Galilee, and the mother of Jesus was there; Jesus also was invited to the marriage, with his disciples. When the wine failed, the mother of Jesus said to him, "They have no wine." And Jesus said to her, "O woman, what have you to do with me? My hour has not yet come." His mother said to the servants, "Do whatever he tells you." Now six stone jars were standing there, for the Jewish rites of purification, each holding twenty or thirty gallons. Jesus said to them, "Fill the jars with water." And they filled them up to the brim. He said to them, "Now draw some out, and take it to the steward of the feast." So they took it. When the steward of the feast tasted the water now become wine, and did not know where it came from (though the servants who had drawn the water knew), the steward of the feast called the bridegroom and said to him, "Every man serves the good wine first; and when men have drunk freely, then the poor wine; but you have kept the good wine until now." This, the first of his signs, Jesus did at Cana in Galilee, and manifested his glory; and his disciples believed in him.*
>
> (John 2:1-11)

I have preached and heard many sermons on this text, but it wasn't until I became a Catholic that I understood the significance of the intercession of Mary. It's hard to miss, but people often do. Some interesting aspects of this that bear mentioning here are:

Mary cares about the issue of the wine. Running out of wine at a wedding in Jewish culture would have been utterly humiliating for the family of the bridegroom. Mary becomes aware of this and decides to act. She didn't tell them, "You guys really blew it. You should've been prepared." She also doesn't try to fix it herself by going out to get more wine. She does what she knows is the best response to this need. She brings it to Jesus.

This is the essence of Mary's intercession: she cares about the lives of people, and intercedes on their behalf by bringing their needs to Jesus. Notice she doesn't beg, plead, or otherwise try to persuade her Son. *She simply states the need.*

But this isn't the end of the story.

Jesus' response to Mary is not arbitrary. He addresses her as "Woman." I used to think this was borderline disrespectful. If a son today answered his mother's request by calling her "woman," it probably wouldn't end well for him. But Jesus was not diminishing her in any way. In fact, He uses this moment as an opportunity to exalt her. When it comes to the Blessed Mother, "Woman" is a special title. This title is first used in Genesis:

> *I will put enmity between you and the woman, and between your offspring and hers; he will strike your head, and you will strike his heel.* (Genesis 3:15 NRSVCE)

Mary is the Woman whose Son crushes the head of the serpent.

Jesus also called her "Woman" during the Crucifixion. In an incredibly tender and beautiful moment, when Jesus saw His mother and the disciple John standing at the foot of the cross, Jesus said to her, "Woman, behold, your son." Then he said to John, "Behold, your mother." (John 19:26-27)

There's still one more reference to Mary in the Scripture that refers to her as "Woman." The disciple John (who lived with Mary for many years, wrote the account of the wedding feast, and heard the words of Jesus at the cross) later described an astounding vision God gave him:

> *And a great portent appeared in heaven, a woman clothed with the sun, with the moon under her feet, and on her head a crown of twelve stars.* (Revelation 12:1)

As these passages show, calling Mary "Woman" has deep meaning for Jesus. He is clearly honoring her. This is proven all the more by how He grants her request—in abundance. The wine He created was more than enough, and it was the best wine of the night. It is powerful that the first "sign" Jesus performed came at the request of His mother.

The spiritual fruit of this mystery is To Jesus Through Mary.
When you meditate on this mystery, think of your needs. It
doesn't matter how trivial they may seem. Whatever you have
"run out of" in your life, bring it to Mary. She cares for you and
knows exactly what to do. She will bring your need to her Son.
And He will respond in an abundance of grace. That grace will
work its way into your life in powerful ways.

Check this out. Jesus didn't just create wine out of nowhere.
He had the servants fill the ceremonial jars with water. Have
you ever wondered why He didn't have them empty the jars
instead? He changed *water* into wine, but why?

Perhaps it's because He wants to show us *how* He purifies us.
This process is echoed in our lives, and it is also echoed in the
Eucharist when the wine is changed into His blood at the Last
Supper. Jesus purifies us by transforming what is natural into
something supernatural. This is not an accident. This is how
He works. Water and wine, you and me. Isn't that awesome?

But wait, there's more. Jesus sees our need and He seeks to
meet it, but He doesn't just meet the need at a base level. The
wine Jesus makes is the *best* wine. Don't miss the power in this.
The words of the Master of the Banquet help us understand the
way Jesus operates compared to the world's way of doing things:

> *Everyone serves good wine first, and then when people have
> drunk freely, an inferior one; but you have kept the good wine
> until now."* (John 2:10 - NABRE)

The world promises everything if we live by its systems. Pleasure, fulfillment, significance, autonomy, and security. But the world lies. Eventually, reality hits, and we find ourselves needing more—but feeling numb. Something just isn't right, so we keep doing more of what doesn't work, foolishly believing that it will. We often repeat this pattern until our wine is gone. That's the world's way.

The way of Jesus is different. The way of Jesus is often harder at first. We struggle. We suffer. We sometimes don't understand. But when it all comes together, we realize that Jesus has saved the best for last. For eternity.

Where in your life have you been drinking the cheap wine of the world? Where have you found yourself empty? Come to Jesus through His Blessed Mother, and He will change the natural into the supernatural. He has indeed saved the best for last.

What does it look like for you to go to Jesus through Mary? Have you been trying to persuade God on your own? Maybe it's time to ask Mary for His help. But how? No matter how large or small your need, simply ask Mary to bring it to Jesus. She brought Him to us. She will bring us to Him if we ask her. And He will work miracles.

THE PROCLAMATION OF THE KINGDOM
Spiritual Fruit—Christian Witness and Conversion

Thy word is a lamp unto my feet
and a light to my path.
(Psalm 119:105)

Can you imagine anything more illuminating than hearing Jesus preach? I've listened to many great preachers deliver impactful, powerful, and life-changing sermons. What makes one sermon better than another? Is it strictly related to the content? What about the charisma of the speaker? Undoubtedly, Jesus had it all. He preached perfectly.

Many people heard Jesus proclaim the Kingdom of Heaven, but not everyone received His words. Why not? Did it have something to do with His delivery? Was He not entertaining or engaging? Was Jesus just a bad preacher? When it comes to the effectiveness of a sermon, are there any other factors that need consideration? I think so. Jesus often said, "He who has ears to hear, let him hear." This means that the effectiveness of a sermon isn't just about the preacher but also the hearer.

Sometimes people just aren't ready to hear a particular message. Lots of people like to talk about what Jesus came to say. Some people say things like, "Jesus came to preach love and unconditional acceptance," or "Jesus came to challenge the establishment." These vague statements may have some elements of truth, but if we truly want to know what Jesus had to say, we must understand that He was, and is, calling the world to conversion.

When He returns from the desert after his Baptism, Jesus preaches about a radical change of heart and life. "Repent for the kingdom of heaven is at hand." (Matthew 4:17) This is a call to conversion. Jesus isn't just giving advice or a new philosophy. He's also not simply telling people to try harder at their religion. He is calling His hearers to be converted, not only in their behavior but in the deepest part of their hearts; to turn from sin, and from relying on their ability to keep all the rules. Jesus showed everyone a new way, a better way, the fullest way to enter into the Kingdom—through faith in Him.

Only a limited number of people had the opportunity to hear Jesus preach personally, but His message continues through the ministry of the Church. As He sent the apostles to do His work, He told them, "He who hears you hears me...." (Luke 10:16) When we hear the words of Jesus through the teaching of the

Church, we hear the Kingdom of Heaven proclaimed. Will we receive it? Will we let it into our hearts to change us?

The spiritual fruit of this mystery is Christian Witness and Conversion. We must be converted or we will not be effective witnesses. What does it mean to be converted? First, you have to put yourself in a position to hear Jesus. How can you *know* what He says if you never really *listen* to what He says? Do you read the Bible? When you go to Mass, do you listen attentively to the readings and homilies? Do you have ears that hear?

But how do we get our ears to hear? We must become completely open to what Jesus says. This means we must stop prioritizing our own opinions or making His words fit our beliefs. Human beings can be very good at rationalizing whatever we want to do or believe. It's easy to convince ourselves that "God will understand." However, Jesus' words leave no room for our self-serving interpretations. If we're honest with ourselves, we can think of many times when Jesus' words contradict our existing worldview. If you truly listen to Jesus, you *will* be challenged. So let Him challenge you.

When you do, He will convert you. This means that your entire being will be centered on your relationship with God—not just following rules or mechanically exercising religious practices. Instead of focusing on ourselves, we will focus entirely on Jesus. Conversion means you're "all in."

When Jesus converts you, it is never just about you. Jesus wants you to light the way for others: "Nor do men light a lamp and put it under a bushel, but on a stand, and it gives light to all in the house." (Matthew 5:15)

How do we show others the truth about Jesus? People often ask me, "What can I say or give to people to bring them to God or back to the Church?" It's a great question. The reality is that a converted heart is our best resource. We share what Jesus shared with our words, but also we *show* what Jesus shared through our converted lives. That doesn't mean we don't say what needs to be said. We have to do both. Show them and tell them. Our witness comes from our conversion. You can't give away what you don't have.

Have you heard the words of Jesus? Have you received the Kingdom proclaimed and been converted? If not, it's time to be illuminated by Jesus so you can light the way for others.

THE TRANSFIGURATION OF JESUS
Spiritual Fruit—Courage

*And after six days Jesus took with him Peter and James
and John, his brother, and led them up a high mountain
apart. And he was transfigured before them, and his
face shone like the sun, and his garments became white
as light. And behold, there appeared to them Moses
and Eli'jah, talking with him. And Peter said to Jesus,
"Lord, it is well that we are here; if you wish, I will make
three booths here, one for you and one for Moses and
one for Eli'jah." He was still speaking, when lo, a bright
cloud overshadowed them, and a voice from the cloud
said, "This is my beloved Son, with whom I am well
pleased; listen to him." When the disciples heard this,
they fell on their faces, and were filled with awe. But
Jesus came and touched them, saying, "Rise, and have
no fear." And when they lifted up their eyes, they saw
no one but Jesus only.*
(Matthew 17:1-8)

The first time I saw the Rocky Mountains of Colorado, I was blown away. I was around twelve and went camping in my parents' pop-up camper in Estes Park. Having been raised in Iowa, the closest thing I'd seen to a real mountain were images on our 15" television. The size and beauty of the landscape dwarfed my expectations.

After a few days, the newness began to wear off, and although I still appreciated the beauty, I was no longer overwhelmed. By the time we headed home after a couple of weeks, I was used to the scenery, and even though I appreciated it, I wasn't as captivated. During the ride home, instead of looking out the window, I read a magazine about my favorite band.

Have you ever experienced anything like this? Sometimes amazing things get taken for granted when we see them every day. This is unfortunate, but it's part of our reality. During a typical day, it's normal to get caught up dealing with the challenges in our lives or in trivial distractions and interests. As a result, we filter out incredible things right in front of us. This mental reflex seems involuntary. And tragically, it robs us of the beauty all around us.

I don't know what it was like to live with Jesus every day for three years. I wonder if the awe and wonder of being with Him faded for His disciples. After all, they continued to argue about trivial things ("Who is the greatest among us?"). They got tired or distracted ("Why could you not keep watch with me for one hour?"). Is it far-fetched to imagine that even Our Lord's closest companions sometimes took Him for granted?

Perhaps *this* is why Jesus was transfigured. He literally *showed them* a greater revelation of Himself because He knew they would need it. He knew harrowing experiences were looming on the near horizon. When they witnessed this incredible illumination, their awe of Jesus overwhelmed them. They hit the ground in fear. Can you blame them?

During the Transfiguration, Peter said, "It is good for us to be here." That's the understatement of the year! Then the voice from heaven declared, "This is my son whom I love; with him I am well pleased. *Listen to him.*" (emphasis mine) We heard this voice in the first Luminous Mystery. The essence of the Luminous Mysteries is summed up in this one command: Listen to Jesus. It's what Mary told the servants at the wedding feast at Cana. It's what we confront when Jesus' proclamation of the Kingdom challenges our beliefs. If you want illumination, you have to *listen* to Jesus. Why? Because He is God!

The spiritual fruit of this mystery is Courage. The Transfiguration reveals to all of us that Jesus is not just another man but is greater than we can imagine. Peter, James, and John were terrified when they heard the voice. What is the next thing Jesus tells them to do? "Rise, and have no fear."

In other words, have courage.

What in your life would change if you listened to Jesus say to you, "Rise and have no fear." I want you to seriously think about this. Ask yourself right now. What comes to mind?

The first part of this Luminous Mystery has to do with information: Jesus is God. The next part has to do with our resolve to be not afraid, to be courageous, and not because we are so great, but because Jesus is so great.

Have you allowed your experience of Jesus to become too familiar? Have you ever found yourself taking Him for granted? This can happen so easily. We attend the Holy Sacrifice of the Mass, and even though a miracle is occurring right before our eyes during the elevation of the Eucharist, we can miss Jesus' glory and power right in front of us. We can become so caught up in our own thoughts that we miss the beauty of Who is with us. Meditating on the Transfiguration of Jesus will help us recover that childlike sense of awe.

In 2014, my parents fulfilled a lifelong dream and purchased a small cabin in the Wet Mountains, southwest of Colorado Springs. I love being there. As I have grown older, I have noticed my sense of awe and wonder has grown—the opposite of what happened to me as a boy. The more time I spend in the mountains, the more my appreciation for the beauty around me increases. Whatever distraction or discontentment is going on in my life, seeing the beauty of the landscape resets my mind.

This same principle applies to our relationship with Jesus. The more we experience how amazing and beautiful He is, the more awestruck we will be at His presence in our lives. I remember watching a video of St. Padre Pio celebrating Mass; he was overwhelmed by the beauty of Jesus in the Eucharist. As he elevated the Sacred Host, his elderly eyes were transfixed on the Lord in amazement. Padre Pio had celebrated Mass thousands of times, but his love of Jesus was so powerful you could see it in his eyes.

As we meditate on the Transfiguration, we must remember we have the privilege to experience a transfiguration every time we attend Mass. Don't miss it! Be overwhelmed. Let the words of Peter be your words as well—"It is good for us to be here."

The Fifth Luminous Mystery

THE INSTITUTION OF THE EUCHARIST
Spiritual Fruit—Love of our Eucharistic Lord

*And as they were eating, he took bread, and blessed,
and broke it, and gave it to them, and said, "Take;
this is my body." And he took a cup, and when he had
given thanks he gave it to them, and they all drank
of it. And he said to them, "This is my blood of the
covenant, which is poured out for many.*

(Mark 14:22-24)

The world has never seen a greater display of love than what we see in the events celebrated in this beautiful mystery. The institution of the Eucharist is about the love Jesus has for all of us. "Greater love has no man than this, that a man lay down his life for his friends."(John 15:13) Jesus did not come merely to show us *the way* to salvation. Jesus *is* the way of salvation. Salvation isn't just a message, it's a person.

Earlier in His ministry, Jesus told His followers,

> *Truly, truly, I say to you, unless you eat the flesh of the Son of man and drink his blood, you have no life in you; he who eats my flesh and drinks my blood has eternal life, and I will raise him up at the last day. For my flesh is food indeed, and my blood is drink indeed. He who eats my flesh and drinks my blood abides in me, and I in him. As the living Father sent me, and I live because of the Father, so he who eats me will live because of me.* (John 6:53-57)

After Jesus said these words, almost all of His followers left Him. They were offended by the insinuation that they needed to do something (eat human flesh) clearly forbidden in Jewish Law. Can you blame them? Taken the wrong way, it sounded strange.

What they failed to grasp was that Jesus was making a reference to the Passover lamb they ate every year. The Feast of the Passover commemorated the events that took place in Exodus 12. God punished Pharaoh for his refusal to let the Israelites go. God told Moses to have the people of Israel apply the blood of a spotless lamb to the doorposts of their homes. As the angel of death moved throughout Egypt taking the lives of every firstborn, when he saw the blood of the lamb, he "passed over" the Israelite homes. Pharaoh, whose own son was taken, finally relented and let the Hebrew slaves go.

What's interesting is that the Israelites also *ate the lamb* which had been sacrificed at the first Passover. Every year thereafter, by the command of God, when the Jews celebrated the feast, they ate the flesh of the lamb. The *meal* had reminded them of all God had done to deliver them from slavery and into the Promised Land.

As we saw in the first Luminous Mystery, John the Baptist was the first person to explicitly refer to Jesus as the Lamb of God. This was the same "lamb" about whom Abraham spoke. This also applies to the Passover lamb. It's clear that God showed us multiple times in the Old Testament that He was prefiguring Jesus as the Lamb. John the Baptist saw this and pointed directly at Christ. "Behold the Lamb of God, who takes away the sin of the world." (John 1:29)

It's unclear when each of the disciples made this connection. How did they understand Jesus' words about eating His flesh and drinking His blood? Did they realize that this Passover meal they would celebrate with Jesus would be the fulfillment of the Passover for all eternity? Did they recognize that Jesus Himself would become the Lamb of God who would set them free—not from political bondage, but from slavery to sin? At what point during the Last Supper did they realize, as they took and ate what appeared to be bread and wine, that they were living out what Jesus taught in John 6? Jesus Himself would become the ultimate sacrifice, and through His sacrifice, He would bring life to the world.

But what we cannot miss is the importance of what Jesus said next, "Do this in remembrance of me."(Luke 22:19) The *this* is the offering of the sacrifice. That was the very moment Jesus ordained the apostles as priests; only priests can offer atonement sacrifices. But why the command *to continue* doing this? It wasn't because the sacrifice needed to be repeated. The book of Hebrews tells us that Jesus was sacrificed "once for all." There are at least three reasons for us to ponder this command when we meditate on the final Luminous Mystery.

First, Jesus wants us to *remember* what He has done for us. God told the Jews to celebrate Passover every year so they wouldn't forget what God had done for them. Followers of Jesus also need to remember what He has done for us.

Second, we remember what God has done for us *so we can be thankful.* In fact, the Greek word *eucharist* literally means *thanksgiving.* When the followers of Jesus celebrate the Eucharist at Mass, we give thanks to God by obeying the command of Jesus to eat His flesh and drink His blood.

Third, although His sacrifice happened once for all, through the Eucharist, Jesus perpetually fulfills His promise to remain with the Church. (Matthew 28:20) During the Holy Sacrifice of the Mass, when the host is consecrated by the priest, Jesus is literally present with us. He never leaves us. What an act of love! And what is our response to this act of love?

The spiritual fruit of this mystery is Love of our Eucharistic Lord. That's what Jesus wants. What does it mean to love Jesus in the Eucharist? Jesus tells us exactly: "If you love me, you will keep my commandments."(John 14:15) These words were spoken by Jesus just before He instituted the Eucharist.

What should we make of this? How is keeping a command related to love? We can't say what Jesus said without getting into trouble. For example, if we told someone they had to obey our commands if they loved us, they would probably laugh. This is because we are flawed human beings with selfish motives. We might believe we would only tell others to do something which was good for them, but this presumes we can actually know what is good for them in all circumstances. We don't, but Jesus does. Jesus knows what is good for us *and* loves us perfectly; therefore, anything He commands of us is the best thing for us.

In order to believe that, first we have to love Him. Loving Jesus isn't just about thinking He's awesome. As we see above, loving Jesus is about submitting ourselves to Him and obeying His commands.

However, it's easy to mess this up by reducing His commands to merely following rules. This is a common trap among religious people. If we believe that Jesus came just to give us better rules to follow, we will miss the gospel. Jesus saves us because He loves us, and His desire is for us to love Him back. Because He loves us, He has given us the best way to live. That's where His commands come in. We were made for a relationship with God; therefore, we must not offend God through sin. If you want to be in a loving relationship with someone, you cannot knowingly do things to offend them. Obedience without love does not cut it, just as love without obedience does not work. Don't miss this!

Where does this intersect with your life? Every time you go to Mass, begin by thanking God for what He has done.

Then, increase your level of thanksgiving when you receive Jesus in the Eucharist. In addition to Mass, spend more time in Eucharistic Adoration just loving Jesus. As you become aware of any commands that you are *not* obeying, it's time to change your ways. Don't change out of fear of breaking the rules, but out of love for the one who offered Himself for you.

Finally, to enjoy the spiritual fruit of Love of Our Eucharistic Lord, we must always remember that Jesus told us to "do this in memory of me." It is easy to *forget to remember.* Even as we attend Mass and receive the Eucharist, the temptation is there to remember anything and everything *except* Jesus. We can daydream or think about our tasks or worries instead. Or we waste our focus on what others are doing (or not doing). We can go through the motions while not giving Jesus a second thought.

Loving Jesus must include remembering what He has done for us *every time* we receive the Eucharist. Next time you go to Mass, as you prepare to receive the body and blood of Jesus, tell Him, "Thank you Jesus. I love you." Repeat this from the moment you leave your pew until you return after receiving Him. I promise you will never forget to remember to love our Eucharistic Lord.

Closing Thoughts

on The Luminous Mysteries

The Luminous Mysteries bring light to areas of our faith where a darkened understanding can lead to spiritual stagnation, and sadly, a lack of love for God. When we allow the light of these mysteries to reveal the truth, guide us, and comfort us, we will experience the fullness of our faith. We can recognize who Jesus is and allow Him to guide us into amazing things we would never choose for ourselves. When the light shines, we become aware of the beauty of the truth that we are truly loved and not alone. We learn there are miracles in store for us—miracles above and beyond what we deserve! Exploring all that Jesus reveals to us in these mysteries is the only thing that can really change us—which will in turn change the world.

The life of an illuminated disciple will take us into uncharted waters. We will need courage and fearlessness. That's exactly what we will receive. Most of all, we will remember that we are loved by a God who has proven His love by laying down His life for us. And we will learn what it means to love Him back. That love will chase away even the blackest darkness in the universe.

Part Three

THE SORROWFUL MYSTERIES

He was despised and rejected by men; a man of
sorrows, and acquainted with grief; and as one
from whom men hide their faces he was despised,
and we esteemed him not. Surely he has borne our
griefs and carried our sorrows; yet we esteemed
him stricken, smitten by God, and afflicted.
(Isaiah 53:3-4)

When I was a youth pastor, the church I served took part in a community-wide Good Friday service. Around a dozen churches from various denominations formed a team of pastors to plan it. We discussed which readings to use and songs to sing. Each church would have a reader or leader responsible for individual elements of the service. I proposed having a live-action crucifixion scene outside the church building so that people would encounter something impactful when they left the service. The plan involved three life-sized crosses planted in the ground. On each cross, a man covered in fake blood and dirt would hang to create a three-dimensional visual of the events of Good Friday. "Roman guards" would stand beneath the crosses with torches to illuminate the scene. Finally, when we all exited the church, this depiction of what Jesus had done for us would have an unforgettable impact.

I was convinced this was a great idea. Unfortunately, some of the other leaders didn't agree.

"My people aren't ready for that kind of death and sadness," one pastor remarked, looking around the room. He was offended. I was shocked. Others nodded in agreement, adding to my surprise.

Into this crazy scene, my senior pastor Craig interjected, "But this is what Good Friday is all about! If your people aren't ready for it, it's your job to get them there."

Because we were hosting the service, Craig and I had a little more pull. Half the pastors boycotted and held their own service. For the people in churches that remained, it was amazing—a powerful ending to an incredible Good Friday. I still can't forget it.

No one enjoys sorrow. But to truly follow Jesus, we must be willing to enter into the tough stuff. The Sorrowful Mysteries help us understand the extreme lengths Jesus went for our salvation.

I recently had a fascinating conversation on my podcast with the well-known author, Father Michael Gaitley. At one point, I sensed the Holy Spirit prompting me to ask a question about something which had been puzzling me for months.

"Father, do you think it's possible, through our prayers, to console Jesus in the Garden? I know this was in the past, but God is outside of time. Maybe it's a crazy idea. I'm just crushed every time I think of Jesus in the Garden going through this pain alone."

Fr. Michael hesitated, then asked, "Keith, have you ever heard of my book, *Consoling the Heart of Jesus?* That's what it's all about."

I was embarrassed to admit I had never heard of his book, yet we were both blown away by how the Holy Spirit moved in this conversation. The Sorrowful Mysteries invite us into what Jesus went through for us. It will never be enjoyable, but it's important. We need to follow Jesus anywhere He goes. Especially to the cross.

THE AGONY IN THE GARDEN
Spiritual Fruit—God's Will be Done

Then Jesus went with them to a place called Gethsémane, and he said to his disciples, "Sit here, while I go yonder and pray." And taking with him Peter and the two sons of Zeb'edee, he began to be sorrowful and troubled. Then he said to them, "My soul is very sorrowful, even to death; remain here, and watch with me." And going a little farther he fell on his face and prayed, "My Father, if it be possible, let this cup pass from me; nevertheless, not as I will, but as thou wilt." And he came to the disciples and found them sleeping; and he said to Peter, "So, could you not watch with me one hour? Watch and pray that you may not enter into temptation; the spirit indeed is willing, but the flesh is weak."

(Matthew 26:36-41)

The Last Supper was over. The Lord had washed the disciples' feet. Jesus had taught them so many things that night, which culminated in the Institution of the Eucharist. They sang a hymn. Jesus went to the garden. The disciples fell asleep. Jesus was alone now, contemplating what lay ahead for Him. He always knew this day would come. He humbly asked the Father if it was possible to accomplish the plan for salvation in another way. He was under such distress, that he began to sweat drops of blood.

It's difficult to think about Jesus this way—to imagine Him afraid and full of dread. Most of us experience anxiety over what *might* happen to us, but Jesus knew what *would* happen. He knew how painful it would be. So He cries out to His Father. Crying out to the Father is what He had taught His disciples to do. When fear overcame them as they faced death on the boat during the storm, Jesus rebuked them, "Why are you afraid? Have you no faith?" (Mark 4: 35-41) On that very night in the garden, He had assured them, "Let not your hearts be troubled." (John 14:1) Now, here is Jesus, overcome by sorrow and trouble. How does this make sense? How could He ask for a way out? The Book of Hebrews provides insight:

> *For we have not a high priest who is unable to sympathize with our weaknesses, but one who in every respect has been tempted as we are, yet without sin.*　　　(Hebrews 4:15)

Sometimes the biggest temptations in life do not involve pleasure or power. Sometimes they are about fear. Sometimes we are tempted to play it safe, to turn away from the agony that obedience to God can bring. We must not forget that Jesus was both fully God and fully human. Jesus might have been tempted to call down legions of angels to protect Himself. Or He could have simply walked away. Jesus would experience the full force of the pain, and He knew it.

Yet, His overriding desire was to follow the will of the Father, "not as I will, but as thou wilt." This was His prayer, and even in this victory in the garden over the evil one, Jesus' pain remained. His need for consolation remained. "Could you not keep watch with me for one hour?" He pleaded to His oblivious disciples. Even though they were unwilling to be with Him, Jesus was not without consolation—an angel came and strengthened Him.

When you submit your will to the will of the Father, scary things can happen. This is because God's will doesn't always take suffering off the table. In fact, submission to the will of God often *invites* suffering. One of the most important realizations about being a Christian is accepting what Jesus told the disciples: "In this world you will have trouble." (John 16:33 - NABRE) The choice we all must make is whether we will follow the will of the Father when the trouble comes.

As His Passion began, Jesus passed through immeasurable suffering *before* anyone had even laid a hand on Him. We are called to imitate His example when our suffering comes. And it will. Like Jesus, may we cry out, "Thy will be done!"

The spiritual fruit of this mystery is God's Will Be Done. This is fitting for beginning the Sorrowful Mysteries. In general, we don't want to suffer, and it's okay to admit that. But sometimes, following God's will for our lives puts us right in the middle of suffering. How do we reconcile the paradox? If God loves us and only wants what's best for us, why doesn't He keep us from suffering?

The answer to this question is why this is called a "mystery." It's not something easily understood, but what we will find in Jesus' experience is that sometimes suffering is necessary for reasons known only to God. And the fact that Jesus Himself went straight into His suffering shows us that He isn't calling us to do anything He hasn't already done. Jesus has been there. Jesus understands our suffering because He suffered. Whatever kind of suffering we encounter in this life, Jesus gets it. We have to get over the false idea that if we just do the will of God, then everything will be great, and we can avoid suffering.

The lives of the saints offer countless examples of men and women whose obedience to the will of God led them right into the mouth of suffering. This experience was literally true for men like St. Ignatius of Antioch, who was fed to lions in the Roman Colosseum because of his faith. St. Maximilian Kolbe gave his life in the Nazi death camp, Auschwitz, to save the life of another man who had a family. Many other saints experienced similar fates. If we want to follow God's will, we have to be willing to accept *whatever* happens.

This isn't to say that you will be miserable every time you obey God. Following Jesus and living a holy life will save you from much pain, but it can also invite much pain, including rejection from loved ones, denial of worldly pleasures, and giving up what you want for the good of others. These things involve suffering, but because God has a plan—it's worth it.

What does submission to the Father's will look like for you? Are there areas of your life where you are afraid to follow God because of the consequences? What would it look like for you to face the hard stuff in order to embrace God's will? Maybe a relationship has to end. Perhaps you will have to come clean about some failure. You might have to disappoint some people. Or maybe you will miss out on something sinful that others around you are enjoying.

When I was in seminary, there was a man who left a lucrative career in entertainment because his faith demanded it. Later, God called him to become a pastor. He had once made millions, but left it all behind. It wasn't easy for him, but he obeyed God's will.

Are you willing to walk into suffering, like Jesus, to do the will of God? The Agony in the Garden shows us that it will not be easy. And the fact that it's difficult doesn't mean God doesn't love you, or even that you have done anything wrong. Suffering comes. Agony comes. Will you cry out, "Thy will be done"? Will you console the heart of Jesus in His agony? Meditating on the Agony in the Garden does exactly that.

Even in the midst of suffering, God will not leave you. He will send His angels to *strengthen* you. There are few things more powerful in this world than a disciple of Jesus who is prepared to follow God's will into suffering.

Sin entered the world in a garden when the first Adam chose to follow his own will, rather than obey God. It was only fitting that the events of the Passion of the Lord also began in a garden. Jesus, the New Adam (1 Corinthians 15:45), willingly submits Himself to the will of the Father to reverse the consequences of Adam's disobedience.

Which Adam will you follow?

THE SCOURGING AT THE PILLAR
Spiritual Fruit—Purity

But he was wounded for our transgressions, he was bruised for our iniquities; upon him was the chastisement that made us whole, and with his stripes we are healed.

(Isaiah 53:5)

After Jesus was arrested in the Garden of Gethsemane, the mob took Him to the home of Caiaphas, the High Priest. There He was falsely accused of blasphemy and condemned. However, the Jewish religious leaders did not have the political authority to kill Jesus. Only the occupying Romans could sentence someone to death. So the Jewish leaders took Jesus to see the regional governor, Pontius Pilate. Jewish religious squabbles did not concern him. Their issues with Jesus were nothing more than an annoyance. Pilate was a pagan who worshiped the Roman gods, including the emperor Caesar, who had proclaimed himself a god. And Caesar was his boss. Pilate's primary concern was keeping the peace in a troublesome province.

During the Feast of Passover, the city of Jerusalem swelled beyond its normal population. Pilate had placed the Roman soldiers on high alert. The last thing he wanted was an uprising. When Caiaphas and his crew dragged Jesus before him, they held the threat of violence and revolt over Pilate to get their way.

At first, Pilate didn't seem interested in executing Jesus. He questioned Jesus, and Our Lord's answers led Pilate to believe that Jesus had done nothing deserving death. Pilate then told the growing crowd: "You brought me this man as one who was perverting the people; and after examining him before you, behold, I did not find this man guilty of any of your charges against him...nothing deserving death has been done by him. I will therefore chastise him and release him." (Luke 23:14-16)

The Jewish mob was furious! They wanted Jesus dead. Pilate hoped a compromise was possible. To appease them, he decided to have Jesus beaten and then released. If Pilate believed Jesus was innocent, why punish Him? He wanted the people to fear him, but because justice was important to the Romans, he did not want to execute an innocent man, so Jesus was taken to be scourged.

Roman beatings were notoriously cruel and brutal. The victim was tied to a pillar, stripped, and repeatedly lashed with horrible whips designed to inflict massive damage. This is what happened to Jesus.

When we visualize Jesus tied to the whipping post, we must remember that He allowed this to happen. He had the power to summon angels to free Him at any moment. He could have ended the pain with a simple act of His will.

The idea that Jesus was secured to the pillar by chains is an illusion. The only thing that held Jesus in place was His love for His Father and for humanity. Hundreds of years before Jesus was born, Isaiah had prophesied about this event.

> *Surely he has borne our griefs and carried our sorrows; yet we esteemed him stricken, smitten by God, and afflicted. But he was wounded for our transgressions, he was bruised for our iniquities; upon him was the chastisement that made us whole, and with his stripes we are healed. All we like sheep have gone astray; we have turned every one to his own way; and the Lord has laid on him the iniquity of us all.*
>
> (Isaiah 53:4-6)

As the whips crossed the back of Jesus over and over, stripes of blood appeared, and with them came the healing of humanity. How was this possible?

The spiritual fruit of this mystery is Purity. At first glance, this fruit seems confusing. How does an innocent man's unjust, brutal torture lead to purity? To understand the connection, we must remember why Jesus came to earth. In Matthew's Gospel, the angel of the Lord appeared to Joseph in a dream and told him to name the child *Jesus* because "he will save his people from their sins." (Matthew 1:21)

Jesus told His followers that He would suffer and die throughout the gospels. "Behold, we are going up to Jerusalem; and the Son of man will be delivered to the chief priests and scribes, and they will condemn him to death, and deliver him to the Gentiles to be mocked and scourged and crucified..." (Matthew 20:18-19)

Jesus' Passion was not a surprise to Him. This was the reason He came to earth. The sin of humanity demanded punishment to satisfy God's wrath. God knew that human beings could never atone for their sins. Out of love, God sent His only begotten Son to take on the punishment for them. The crucial thing to understand is that Jesus is not an unwilling victim. Jesus explained this to His disciples, "For this reason the Father loves me, because I lay down my life, that I may take it again. No one takes it from me, but I lay it down of my own accord. I have power to lay it down, and I have power to take it again; this charge I have received from my Father." (John 10:17-18)

God was not appeased *just* because Jesus suffered, but because Jesus *willingly* sacrificed Himself. For the redemption of the world to occur, there must be a willing act of perfect love. In the Garden of Eden, Adam and Eve willingly acted in disobedience against God. As a result, the world was plunged into darkness and bondage. When Jesus sacrificed himself, He brought light and freedom.

This willingness reveals why the spiritual fruit of the second sorrowful mystery is Purity. Jesus' willingness to endure this torture removed the punishment we are owed because of our sin. We have been *made pure* by His blood because He was both free from sin and offered Himself freely, "...the blood of Jesus his Son cleanses us from all sin." (1 John 1:7)

To be pure means that our sins have been washed away by the blood of Jesus. This purity is not something we can accomplish for ourselves. It is something done for us and *to us*. Why does this matter? If we fall into the trap of believing that our purity comes from our own efforts, we will become self-reliant. We will think our purity is about us. This mindset can result in self-righteous pride (when we believe we have succeeded) or self-loathing hopelessness (when we realize we have failed).

However, when we rightly rely on the sacrifice of Jesus for our purity, we cultivate an attitude of humility, gratitude, and love. When you love Jesus, you will want to please Him, even when it's tough, even when it means denying yourself. When you love Jesus, you will obey His commands, which guide you into holiness and obedience. The result is purity.

Purity comes from Jesus, but we must walk in it. When we willingly turn away from Jesus, we forfeit what He has done for us at the pillar. Just as it required an act of the will by Jesus to suffer for us, an act of the will on our part is required to receive this purity.

What does that look like for you? How does meditating on this mystery help you walk in purity?

Perhaps, it is a matter of recognizing the pain Jesus suffered on your behalf, which can help us learn the true price for our salvation.

The next time you are tempted with sin, imagine the Lord strapped to the pillar. Imagine yourself holding the whip. To willingly sin is to inflict another blow on His back. Will you strike Him or put the whip down and console Him instead?

Perhaps meditating on this mystery will help you become pure because you have felt like a failure. You've done your best to be a good person. You've kept the rules, but you still feel like a failure. Even though you have stayed "pure on the outside," on the inside, you have fostered thoughts you aren't proud of. No matter how hard you try, you can't shake the feeling that you will never be good enough for God. I can relate to this feeling.

Perhaps the Scourging at the Pillar shows you a love that is beyond anything this world has to offer. This is not a display of physical endurance. The Scourging at the Pillar is a display *of love*. The divine love displayed by Jesus could cause you to look upon Him with so much love that the junk of this world will lose its appeal. When you realize how loved you are, nothing else can compare.

Meditating on this mystery reminds us that we can't make ourselves pure. We can't do this on our own. Jesus' sacrifice was necessary, and He did it. Your purity is not the result of your willpower, but comes from what He has done. Receive it and become pure.

THE CROWNING WITH THORNS
Spiritual Fruit—Reign of Christ in our Hearts

It can be difficult to submit ourselves to others. Last year, I went to the doctor, and she told me I needed to lose weight. My blood pressure was too high, my liver readings were elevated, and according to some stupid chart, I was overweight. How dare it say that? I've always been in decent shape.

Like many people, 2020 wasn't my healthiest year, but I didn't think much of it. I had to face the reality that I had become a middle-aged fat dude. I decided it was time to get back to being healthy, but I needed help. I enlisted my friend Joe, a professional trainer and a Catholic convert like me. He's tall and super fit (I'm 5'7" on a good day). I had already been lifting at his gym for several months, and although I was getting stronger, I was also packing on useless pounds. Apparently, you can still get fat if you eat too many tacos no matter how many squats and deadlifts you do. I told Joe that I needed to get serious about losing some weight. After that doctor's visit, I was really worried.

Joe asked if I was willing to follow a strict nutrition program. It was something called a "protein sparing fast." Basically, you can eat anything you want as long as it's a boneless, skinless, tasteless chicken breast. I could also eat green veggies without any butter. No fat. No carbs. No satisfaction.

However, I was determined to follow the plan. It wasn't easy. At first, every night I was tempted to eat something besides that chicken. If I had been good for a few days, surely I deserved a reward, right? A slice (or three) of pizza or a scoop (or giant bowl) of ice cream before bed was harmless, right? At least it wasn't tacos.

The only thing that saved me from cheating was that Joe's program required me to keep track of everything that went into my body. This removed the option of fooling myself into thinking I was doing better than I was. "Everyone thinks they're starving themselves until they track their food," Joe tells everybody. He's right.

When we're in charge of ourselves, we will almost always find excuses to "modify" the program. This is why we need personal trainers and calorie counting. Thankfully, with Joe in charge, I lost the weight. My blood pressure returned to normal, my jeans started to fit again, and now I feel great. It wasn't easy, but it was worth it.

Submitting ourselves to another person can be difficult, but it's often the *only* way to overcome our own weaknesses and shortcomings. If this is true when it comes to our bodies, how much more true is it when it comes to our souls? But who can we trust? The answer is what the Third Sorrowful Mystery is all about.

> *And the soldiers plaited a crown of thorns, and put it on his head, and arrayed him in a purple robe; they came up to him, saying, "Hail, King of the Jews!" and struck him with their hands. Pilate went out again, and said to them, "See, I am bringing him out to you, that you may know that I find no crime in him." So Jesus came out, wearing the crown of thorns and the purple robe. Pilate said to them, "Behold the man!"*
> (John 19:2-5 RSV)

Before this dramatic event, Pilate had asked Jesus,

> *"So you are a king?" Jesus answered, "You say that I am a king. For this I was born, and for this I came into the world, to testify to the truth. Everyone who belongs to the truth listens to my voice."* (John 18:37 - NRSVCE)

As we saw earlier, the Jews attempted to convince Pilate that Jesus was a political threat to Roman rule. Pilate needed to know if Jesus had plans to lead an insurgency. Jewish revolts had caused problems in the past and Pilate was under pressure to prove to his superiors that he could handle things. Religious issues were of little concern to him, but when he heard that Jesus was claiming to be *a king,* he was forced to investigate. Jesus did not respond to Pilate in a way you would expect from someone on trial for his life. He did not plead for mercy. He did not defend Himself.

The Roman soldiers weren't content to inflict only physical pain. They also mocked Jesus; they dressed Him in royal purple and fashioned a crown of thorns, which they forced down into His scalp. The thorns only stopped when they reached Our Lord's skull. What kind of king would allow himself to be abused in such a way? These guards had no fear or respect for Jesus. "Hail, King of the Jews!" (John 19:3) They struck Him repeatedly and laughed. In their minds, their dominance over Him was total.

Pilate then brought Jesus out before the crowd. He had hoped they would be satisfied with the pain and humiliation inflicted upon Him. "Behold, I am bringing him out to you, that you may know that I find no crime in him." (John 19:4) *Would this be enough?* Pilate must have wondered. Was it even possible to appease this bloodthirsty crowd?

Pilate was trying to strike a balance between his Roman sense of justice (after all, he knew Jesus was innocent) while placating this dangerous mob. What would he do with this "king" Jesus?

This is the ultimate question every human being must answer. What will *you* do with King Jesus? When He stands before you, will you acknowledge Him as your king, or will you mock Him? Or will you try to find a middle ground where you can reason with Him without submitting to His authority, like Pilate?

The Third Sorrowful Mystery calls us to recognize Jesus' Kingdom is not a kingdom of this world, but of something far greater. The world's kingdoms are built on dominance and power. This is not the kind of kingdom Jesus desires. All that is required to be a part of a worldly kingdom is to be conquered. The strongest person forces you to submit. Dominance, control, and sheer power define the kings of this world.

Jesus is not that kind of king. Jesus' Kingdom is built on sacrifice, submission, and love. This is the kingdom that each of us is called to, but to receive it, we must freely offer every area of our lives to Jesus. However, His kingdom has no room for tepidity or complacency. It takes grit.

To follow King Jesus, being conquered by a stronger person is not enough. You must choose to love Him. You have to give Him your heart. You can be subject to the kings of the world while hating them at the same time. They don't care if you love them because they *don't love you.* You exist only to keep them in power. King Jesus is different. King Jesus loves you desperately and His most important command for His subjects is *to love Him back.*

The spiritual fruit of this mystery is the Reign of Christ in our Hearts. The best way to incorporate this fruit is to listen to the words of Pilate. When he brings out King Jesus, beaten, bloodied, and crowned in thorns, Pontius Pilate tells the crowd, "Behold, the man."

The crowd saw what had been done to Jesus and they responded, "Crucify, crucify him!" (Luke 23:21)

What will you say when you behold King Jesus? It's a question every human being must answer. Worldly kingdoms are built on reputation, prestige, and comfort. Worldly kings will try to get you to do what they want you to do. Buy their stuff. Accomplish their goals. Put money into their pockets.

For King Jesus to "reign" means there can be no higher authority. There can be no part of you that submits to another kingdom or another king. And the truth is, sometimes human beings function as their own kings. We do what we want, when we want, how we want, and no one can stop us. If we want Jesus to be our king, we must sacrifice membership in every other kingdom. Additionally, we must look within our hearts to make sure we are holding nothing back from Jesus. Where are we making compromises? Where are we making excuses in order to maintain control of some part of our personal kingdom?

As you meditate on this mystery, "Behold, the man." Envision *your* king, Jesus, standing in front of you, a crown on His head. He is inviting you into a kingdom of peace and love. You were made for this kingdom, and for this King. To enter will cost you everything! It's worth it. Jesus is the King *of Kings*. May He be yours as well.

THE CARRYING OF THE CROSS
Spiritual Fruit—The Patient Bearing of Trials

I have decided to follow Jesus.
I have decided to follow Jesus.
I have decided to follow Jesus.
No turning back.
No turning back.
-Nokseng, Indian Martyr

What does it mean to be a Christian? Is being a Christian about ideas you believe? Is being a Christian about living according to certain moral rules? Is anyone who has been baptized set for the rest of his or her life?

The Fourth Sorrowful Mystery shows us an aspect of the Christian faith often neglected in the calls "to be saved" at stadium crusades, parish missions, and youth retreats. How many people at these events would come down to the front—to be nailed to a cross? How many people would raise their hands in response to a call to salvation—if they knew what was coming next was a beating? If we want to be called a "Christian," we must take a closer look at *how* Jesus invited people to follow Him.

When Jesus revealed to the disciples that He would suffer and be killed, Peter rebuked Him. "God forbid, Lord! This shall never happen to you." (Matthew 16:22) You can't blame Peter for not understanding. It doesn't make sense. Jesus is the Son of the Living God. He is more powerful than anyone. How could anyone overpower Him? How could anyone kill Him? Jesus' response to Peter is harsh: "Get behind me, Satan! You are a hindrance to me; for you are not on the side of God, but of men." (Matthew 16:23)

This rebuke addresses an important misconception about the nature of following Christ. Peter believed the plan of God couldn't be compatible with that kind of suffering. Jesus was teaching Peter (and the rest of us) that the center of His mission was to take up a cross and suffer. For Jesus, a wooden cross would be the instrument of suffering that would facilitate the sacrifice to save the world from sin. A cross was necessary for Jesus' mission. Yet before He could be *nailed* to the cross, He had to *carry* it. The Fourth Sorrowful Mystery invites us to be with Jesus on the journey.

> *So they took Jesus, and he went out, bearing his own cross, to the place called the place of a skull, which is called in Hebrew Golgotha.* (John 19:17)

He was exhausted. Blood poured down His face from the thorns piercing His scalp. His back was shredded from whipping. And now He was carrying a heavy beam of wood through the streets of Jerusalem.

How was this even possible? What was going through His mind? As Jesus began, He stumbled and fell. The weight was too much. The soldiers compelled a man named Simon to carry the cross for Him. Tradition tells of an encounter with a woman named Veronica, who wiped His face with a cloth.

His mother was at the foot of the cross, so we know she never left His side during the ordeal. When Jesus looked into her eyes, the anguish she felt for Him undoubtedly caused Him yet another kind of pain. Mary's sorrows had been foretold at the Presentation of Jesus when Simeon prophesied that a sword would pierce her soul. She had known His mission would involve unbearable suffering, and now it was happening. During the carrying of the cross, Mary was right in the middle of it.

As Jesus struggled forward, He saw others who came with Him on this path. "A large number of people followed him, including women who mourned and wailed for him. 'Daughters of Jerusalem, do not weep for me, but weep for yourselves and for your children.'" (Luke 23:27-28)

His words reveal His mindset. Jesus continues to preach the truth to the people. He isn't concerned for Himself, but for *their* souls. There is no room for self-pity or anger. He did not return evil for evil. He didn't complain. He was not impatient. He stayed on mission, knowing that at the end of this road, carrying this cross, He would be nailed to it.

Now that we have focused on Jesus carrying His cross, we must understand what it means for us to carry ours.

The spiritual fruit of this mystery is The Patient Bearing of Trials. After Jesus rebuked Peter, He told His disciples what would be required of them.

> *"...If any man would come after me, let him deny himself and take up his cross and follow me. For whoever would save his life will lose it, and whoever loses his life for my sake will find it."* (Matthew 16:24-25)

Jesus said this long before His followers had any clue about the Crucifixion, but I am sure the meaning became clear as the events of the Passion unfolded. What would taking up their crosses mean for them? For Peter, an actual cross would eventually be carried in Rome. For others, they would follow Jesus into martyrdom in their own way.

For most of us, crucifixion is probably not in the cards. Then what do our crosses look like? In modern society, people often use the term "cross" to refer to anything unpleasant. But just because something is unpleasant, doesn't elevate it to the same category as a "cross" in the way that Jesus means.

How do we know the difference? According to Jesus, a cross is made out of a desire to follow Him and involves the willing loss of one's life for His sake. Does this refer only to instances where people are killed for their faith? Certainly not. Life is filled with crosses that don't involve dying. So how do we know what things count as "crosses" and what things are just the normal difficulties of life? St. Peter's words are extremely helpful in making this distinction.

> *Beloved, do not be surprised at the fiery ordeal which comes upon you to prove you, as though something strange were happening to you. But rejoice in so far as you share Christ's sufferings, that you may also rejoice and be glad when his glory is revealed. If you are reproached for the name of Christ, you are blessed, because the spirit of glory and of God rests upon you. But let none of you suffer as a murderer, or a thief, or a wrongdoer, or a mischief-maker; yet if one suffers as a Christian, let him not be ashamed, but under that name let him glorify God.* (1 Peter 4:12-16)

Isn't it great seeing that St. Peter learned from his rebuke? He shows us the critical distinction is not about *what* the ordeal is, but rather the circumstances and intention of the person undergoing it. For a trial to be considered a "cross," we must enter into it out of a desire to follow Jesus. In essence, we must choose it intentionally or as a direct consequence of our discipleship. For example, St. Jean Brebeuf chose to leave France to evangelize the Indians in Quebec for many years without any normal human comforts. What followed later (two days of torture while he preached and prayed for his tormentors without ceasing) qualifies as a cross because he willingly entered that trial without regard for his life.

But what about those situations that we don't necessarily choose? What about sickness or tragedy? Can we carry these sufferings as crosses too? Absolutely! Most crosses in life are not chosen on the front end. Our trials *become* crosses based on what we do with them. How can we turn our trials into crosses? We begin by orienting our entire lives toward Jesus. When we offer Him everything in our lives, then any suffering we endure can be used by Him for His purpose. St. Paul teaches us how in his letter to the Romans.

> ...*When we cry, "Abba! Father!" it is the Spirit himself bearing witness with our spirit that we are children of God, and if children, then heirs, heirs of God and fellow heirs with Christ, provided we **suffer with him** in order that we may also be glorified with him.*
>
> (Romans 8:15-17, emphasis added)

When we offer our sufferings to God in union with Christ, *any* suffering can be "with him." This happens in the context of our relationship with the Trinity as we present ourselves to God as "living sacrifices", whose lives and missions are united with the cross of Christ. (Romans 12:1) St. Paul continues with this idea in his letter to the Galatians.

> *I have been crucified with Christ; it is no longer I who live, but Christ who lives in me; and the life I now live in the flesh I live by faith in the Son of God, who loved me and gave himself for me.* (Galatians 2:20)

When we give everything in our lives to Jesus, everything that happens can be used for God's purposes, even our trials. This is why the spiritual fruit of this mystery is so critical. If we fail to endure our trials patiently, we will have wasted them. The moment we give in to self-pity or become impatient, we are no longer united with Christ.

We become like Peter and rebuke Jesus: "God forbid, Lord—this shall never happen *to me.*" We have to reject the idea that following Jesus and suffering are incompatible.

It's not just enough to suffer; we must suffer as Christ suffered. We must unite our bodies *and* our attitudes and thoughts.

Does this seem overwhelming? You might look at all the pain and tragedy of life and ask yourself, *Not only do I have to endure it, but now I have to have a good attitude?* I get it.

Another critical aspect of the Fourth Sorrowful Mystery that we often miss is that Jesus didn't endure this journey alone. Simon the Cyrene helped Him by physically carrying the cross. Mary and the others who followed Him helped Him by giving Him emotional support and love. If Jesus needed others to carry His cross, what does it say about us? We need each other. We are not called by God to endure the trials of life alone. We are all connected.

If one member suffers, all suffer together; if one member is honored, all rejoice together. Now you are the body of Christ and individually members of it. (1 Corinthians 12:26-27)

When you are carrying a heavy cross, look to those around you for assistance the way Jesus did. Yet asking for help carrying the cross can be difficult. There are various reasons, including pride, embarrassment, or not wanting to burden others.

For instance, when I served as a senior pastor in a small evangelical church, a woman asked me to pray for her husband's serious illness. Our church had a small prayer meeting the next day, so I assured her I would ask others to intercede for him. She became agitated and interrupted, "Under no circumstances! This is private." I asked her why, and she replied that it was none of their business.

Some people are hesitant to let others know about their trials. We may think keeping our crosses private is a way of not bothering others, but in reality, we are robbing them of their God-given calling. Sometimes the best thing you can do for another person is to allow them to help you. If Jesus needed help, so do you.

And just as we need help carrying *our* burdens, we must help others carry *theirs*. When we see another person bearing a burden, we need to show up. We need to be eager to jump in. In my time in ministry, when people experience tragedy, a period of isolation sometimes follows. Friends and family don't know what to do, so they stay away. People don't know what to say, so they say nothing. This is unacceptable. We need to enter into the trials and crosses of others, whether we feel qualified or not. I can tell you from personal experience that sometimes the most powerful thing someone can do is simply to be present. *Everyone* can do this. Go to them. Pick up the phone. Make time to visit. Bring that meal. Listen to them. Pray with them. Whatever God tells you, do it.

As disciples of Jesus, we must offer ourselves to one another in whatever way Christ asks of us. In doing so, we fulfill the law of Christ. Saint Paul puts it plainly:

> *Bear one another's burdens, and so fulfill the law of Christ.*
> (Galatians 6:2)

We are almost to the end of our journey through the Sorrowful Mysteries. As we walk with Jesus through His Passion, we are coming to a fuller understanding of what it means to be a Christian. When we consider the Fourth Sorrowful Mystery in light of Jesus' words about what it means to follow Him, we learn that being a Christian isn't just about believing certain truths or living a moral lifestyle. Being a Christian is about being a follower of Jesus. Where does He lead us?

To the cross.

> *The world behind me, the cross before me; The world behind me, the cross before me; The world behind me, the cross before me; No turning back, no turning back.*
> -Nokseng, Indian Martyr

THE CRUCIFIXION
Spiritual Fruit—The Pardoning of Injuries

*who, though he was in the form of God, did not
count equality with God a thing to be grasped,
but emptied himself, taking the form of a servant,
being born in the likeness of men. And being found
in human form he humbled himself and became
obedient unto death, even death on a cross.*

(Philippians 2:6-8)

A t the end of the long road with the heavy cross, Jesus was nailed to it. As this was happening, He prayed, "Father, forgive them; for they know not what they do." (Luke 23:34)

The Roman soldiers hammered nails through His hands and feet. Then they raised Him up in an act of brutality and dominance to fulfill Jesus' own words:

> *"And as Moses lifted up the serpent in the wilderness, so must the Son of man be lifted up, that whoever believes in him may have eternal life."* (John 3:14-15)

There He is, raised up for us. Will you look upon Him in faith? Will you follow Him to the end? Will you hear His words from up on the Cross, "I thirst," and understand that He thirsts for you. He thirsts for your love. He thirsts for your healing.

During hours of crucifixion, He never takes a break from His mission. He doesn't have "me time." He is always focused on the Father's will.

This is what the Rosary is all about—it drives us to the foot of the cross. And this is why it is a weapon for our times.

The Sorrowful Mysteries have taken us on this journey beginning in the Garden, reflecting on the agony that Jesus felt even before anyone had struck Him. We saw His trial, where He was falsely accused but did not defend Himself. He was beaten and brutalized at the pillar by repeated lashings. Though He is the King of Kings, He received a crown of thorns. Next, we went with Him on the long, painful journey through the city as Jesus carried the sin of the world in the wood of the cross.

And now, on the cross, we finally come face-to-face with what our disobedience, selfishness, pride, and all our other sins have cost Him. His life.

"It is finished"; and he bowed his head and gave up his spirit.

(John 19:30)

Jesus is dead.

To the world, this looked like the end for Jesus. It was an end indeed—an end to a religious system that didn't really work. The curtain in the Temple that separated the Holy of Holies from the people was torn from top to bottom. There was now no need for a human high priest to offer sacrifices there, because our true High Priest had entered into the real Holy of Holies in heaven, not with the blood of a bull, but with His own blood. (Hebrews 9:12-14) He had no sin of His own to atone for, and thus He atoned for ours, once and for all—finished. Forgiven. Healed.

The spiritual fruit of this mystery is the Pardoning of Injuries. We don't always think of sin as an injury, but that's exactly what it is. Our souls were created for union with God, but sin damages that union. In the case of mortal sin, it kills it.

Sin isn't just about broken rules; it's about broken relationship. When we sin, we turn our backs on God. In the end, if we stay turned away, we will remain separated from God forever. Jesus came to restore our relationship with the Father. Through His death on the cross, Jesus seeks us out and offers grace to us. Whatever our sins, Jesus forgives. Jesus heals.

What does it look like for you to receive that healing? Have you relied on what Jesus accomplished on the Cross? Or do you feel stuck in shame? On the Cross, Jesus did what you and I could never do. Now the question is: Do you want to be made well?

John's Gospel tells of a man who had been paralyzed for *thirty-eight years*. Jesus asked him, "Do you want to be made well?"

It's a yes or no question, but after all those decades, the man was confused. In so many words, he told Jesus, "No one is helping me. I'm stuck."

Then Jesus told him, "Rise, take up your mat and walk."

The man obeyed and was healed. (John 5:2-9)

Why did Jesus ask that question? It's obvious that anyone who is injured would want to be made well, right? When it comes to our own need for healing, we can get confused too.

To receive the healing Jesus offers from the Cross, first we must *want* it. I've met plenty of people who didn't want to be healed. I once knew of a man who knew the truth about Jesus, but had become so wrapped up in his sin that he didn't feel worthy of God's love anymore. So he dove deeper into sin and despair until he took his own life.

He had plenty of chances to change, but in the end, he chose slavery to sin rather than freedom in Christ. When we are overcome by sin, there can be a kind of darkness that washes over us and takes away even our desire for healing. We must remember that the call to healing is a call to the restoration of a relationship with Jesus. Without Him, we can never find healing. With Him, no matter what we have done, we can be healed and forgiven.

When Jesus asks you if you want to be made well, say "Yes." Pick up your mat and be healed.

Not only can Jesus heal us from sins *we* have committed, but He will also deliver us from the sins *others* have committed against us. But to receive this kind of healing, we must forgive. Jesus tells us that our unforgiveness stands in the way of our healing. As we pray in the Our Father, "Forgive us our trespasses as we forgive those who trespass against us."

This willingness to extend forgiveness to others is not optional. Jesus reiterated to His followers, "For if you forgive men their trespasses, your heavenly Father also will forgive you; but if you do not forgive men their trespasses, neither will your Father forgive your trespasses."(Matthew 6:15)

You are mistaken if you think you can receive healing from Jesus while continuing to drink the poison of withholding forgiveness. However, when you let Jesus' grace cover the sins committed against you, then you will experience healing beyond whatever you can imagine.

What do you need to do to make this a reality? The best place to begin is to make an examination of conscience and go to the Sacrament of Confession. Let the grace of Jesus through His priest wash over and heal you.

Maybe it's time for that phone call with that person who hurt you (or the other way around). Bury the hatchet. Offer forgiveness. Stop waiting for something to happen or for someone else to make the first move. Don't be paralyzed any longer. Take up your mat and make peace. Be healed.

Closing Thoughts

on The Sorrowful Mysteries

The Sorrowful Mysteries take us on the most important journey in history. Although the journey was taken by Jesus two thousand years ago, we are invited to join Him every day of our lives. Walking this journey is tough. The Sorrowful Mysteries are not for "advanced" or "radical" Christians. They are for every Christian. The Sorrowful Mysteries are not optional for those who want to follow Jesus. We must go where Jesus went, and do what Jesus did, to rightly be called His disciples.

Our salvation is a free gift from God, but this gift was not without cost. Jesus paid with His flesh and blood, but also with His will. He chose this. And our discipleship requires our choice. Our flesh. Our blood. Meditating on the Sorrowful Mysteries is an invitation to make a choice to suffer. Why would anyone choose to suffer? The answer for the followers of Jesus is that it is through our suffering that we are united to Christ's suffering. It is an answer that will never be popular, but it is the most important message ever proclaimed. St. Paul sums it up best:

When I came to you, brethren, I did not come proclaiming to you the testimony of God in lofty words or wisdom. For I decided to know nothing among you except Jesus Christ and him crucified. And I was with you in weakness and in much fear and trembling; and my speech and my message were not in plausible words of wisdom, but in demonstration of the Spirit and of power, that your faith might not rest in the wisdom of men but in the power of God.

(1 Corinthians 2:1-5)

Part Four

THE GLORIOUS MYSTERIES

The Glorious Mysteries are about what happens when God gets His way. Spoiler alert: In the end, God wins. Following Jesus doesn't mean your life will ever be easy, but it does mean that your life will be meaningful because, despite the challenges of this world, God has a plan! One of my favorite texts in the Bible is John 16:33: "In the world you have tribulation; but be of good cheer, I have overcome the world." Jesus is telling His followers that despite their struggles, they can be positive and joyful because He has already overcome the world. Even when things seem hopeless, because of what we celebrate in the Glorious Mysteries, we can be assured that in the end, nothing can overcome Jesus. This matters because we need to live as people who aren't controlled by fear.

When you look around at the condition of the world, it's easy to become hopeless. We often view reality through the lens of our own circumstances (which may or may not lead us into joy). Life in Christ is different. The reason why is because when we focus on Jesus we see His glory revealed as one who has overcome the world, and even the grave. Furthermore, Jesus has promised us that we can become partakers in His glory through the work He has done. "To this he called you through our gospel, so that you may obtain the glory of our Lord Jesus Christ." (2 Thessalonians 2:14)

When I was learning to ride a motorcycle, the course instructor told us over and over, "where the eyes look, the bike follows." If you are going around a curve, you need to look ahead to where you want to be, not directly at what's in front of you. It takes practice to ride this way, but it works. The Glorious Mysteries help us take our eyes off the world and our own circumstances, and focus on Someone greater who is worthy of all our love, devotion, and honor. Where our eyes look, our souls will follow. It takes practice to live this way. Praying the Glorious Mysteries of the Rosary is a great way to roll.

THE RESURRECTION OF JESUS
Spiritual Fruit—Faith

And very early on the first day of the week they went to the tomb when the sun had risen. And they were saying to one another, "Who will roll away the stone for us from the door of the tomb?" And looking up, they saw that the stone was rolled back; for it was very large. And entering the tomb, they saw a young man sitting on the right side, dressed in a white robe; and they were amazed. And he said to them, "Do not be amazed; you seek Jesus of Nazareth, who was crucified. He has risen, he is not here; see the place where they laid him. But go, tell his disciples and Peter that he is going before you to Galilee; there you will see him, as he told you."

(Mark 16:2-7)

I often have discussions with people about why they should become a Christian. These conversations can take many twists and turns, but people often make it more complex than it needs to be. Some people want to analyze Jesus' teaching in light of their own opinions to see if it "works" for them. Others look at the moral codes and politics of certain Christians to judge if they would fit in with them. Still, others want to make sure that Christianity won't cramp their lifestyle or divert them from their goals.

"That's way too complicated," I tell people.

There's only one reason a person should be a Christian. Christianity is true. Consequently, if Christianity isn't true, there's *no good reason* to be a Christian. It all boils down to this. How can we know if the claims of Christianity are true? This is the fundamental question. The Bible makes this claim, and it hinges upon the Resurrection of Jesus. Here's how the Apostle Paul puts it...

> *"...if Christ has not been raised, then our preaching is in vain and your faith is in vain."* (1 Corinthians 15:14)

That's a pretty bold statement. Especially because he said this when Christ's Resurrection could have been easily disproved if it were not true. The location of Jesus' tomb was well known. The disciples and hundreds of other eyewitnesses claimed to encounter Jesus for weeks after He rose from the dead. Were they all lying? The only thing any skeptic needed to prove Paul and every other Christian wrong was the dead body of Jesus.

"But what if the disciples *stole* the body?" Well, no one dies for a lie. The persecution of Christians by both the pagans and Jews was intense. Surely one of these hundreds of witnesses would have caved rather than go to jail, be beaten, or killed for what they knew was not true. That's not what happened. Instead, the first Christians changed everything about their lives because of their faith in the Resurrection.

These are just two of the many arguments for the Resurrection of Jesus. When the evidence is examined, Jesus' Resurrection is almost impossible to deny. That's why Paul has no problem going all-in. He knows it's true. What then are the ramifications? Everything Jesus taught must also be true. The Resurrection proves it. *That's* why a person should be a Christian. It's true.

Besides being true, there are many other benefits to following Jesus, but there will also be many hardships. In the Resurrection, we see the glory of God revealed in a way that demands our devotion, love, obedience, and faith.

The spiritual fruit of this mystery is Faith. The Bible asserts that "without faith it is impossible to please him. For whoever would draw near to God must believe that he exists and that he rewards those who seek him." (Hebrews 11:6)

If we can't please God without faith, then having faith must please God. Indeed our faith can please God so much that He will reward those who seek Him by faith. The Bible defines faith as "... the assurance of things hoped for, the conviction of things not seen." (Hebrews 11:1) This means that even though we live in a time and place where we can't see the resurrected Jesus like the first Christians did, we still believe in Him. This belief is the center of our very lives.

Faith is amazing! Jesus loves it when He sees faith *in action*. In the gospels, there are only two things that ever *amazed* Jesus. Both involved faith. Jesus was amazed when people who were not Jews had faith in Him, such as the Centurion who possessed the greatest faith in all of Israel. (Luke 7:1-10) He was also amazed when people who you would expect to be devoted to God lacked faith. Jesus was even prevented from performing miracles in Nazareth because of their lack of faith.

> *"And he could do no mighty work there, except that he laid his hands upon a few sick people and healed them. And he marveled because of their unbelief."* (Mark 6:5-6)

What would faith in action look like in your life? First, when you have faith, you will experience joy even when your life is filled with difficulty. Jesus came out on top after all He went through in the Sorrowful Mysteries, so nothing can keep you down.

Faith in action also leads to obedience. When I was a brand-new wrestler in high school, I quickly learned to trust my coach. When I ignored him, I got destroyed. When I did what he told me to do, I had a fighting chance. We can all think of similar examples in our own lives.

When it comes to Jesus, all you need to do is obey His commands, which begin with loving God and loving others. If you have faith, you *will* love God and others, even unto death, because Jesus loved you, even unto death, before rising to life. You will rise with Him. God wins, and faith is how you share in that victory.

Finally, ask yourself, when Jesus looks at you, is He amazed at your faith or the lack of it? How can you know? If your faith depends on whether things are going well at any given moment, then it's time to focus on the unchanging, objective reality of His Resurrection. It happened. It's done. He proved He is God. Christianity is true. However, faith is much more than examining and accepting historical evidence. Faith comes through the power of God, especially in the Sacraments. Faith is a gift. Meditating on this mystery allows us to receive it.

THE ASCENSION OF JESUS
Spiritual Fruit—Hope

So when they had come together, they asked him, "Lord, will you at this time restore the kingdom to Israel?" He said to them, "It is not for you to know times or seasons which the Father has fixed by his own authority. But you shall receive power when the Holy Spirit has come upon you; and you shall be my witnesses in Jerusalem and in all Judea and Samar'ia and to the end of the earth." And when he had said this, as they were looking on, he was lifted up, and a cloud took him out of their sight. And while they were gazing into heaven as he went, behold, two men stood by them in white robes, and said, "Men of Galilee, why do you stand looking into heaven? This Jesus, who was taken up from you into heaven, will come in the same way as you saw him go into heaven."

(Acts 1:6-11)

After Jesus rose from the dead, the disciples must have thought He would now implement the restoration of the Kingdom of Israel back to its full glory. I imagine them thinking, "Finally, let's get rid of the Romans!" He had conquered death and proven His enemies wrong. Surely, He was ready to make His next move!

And then, He leaves.

What did that feel like for His disciples? It was true that Jesus was prepared to implement the next stage in His plan to restore the Kingdom, but not in the way the disciples expected. Jesus had told them during the Last Supper that He would be with them only a short while. From their perspective, it didn't make sense. Just before He ascends, He makes it clear there are some things they can know and other things they can't.

It's often like that for us. If we were running the show, we would probably do everything differently, but we aren't God. He sees things we do not see. His ways are not our ways. The disciples expected Him to do the heavy lifting, but His plan involved *them* carrying out His mission.

Final words matter. When people say final words, they make sure they count. Think of someone on his deathbed or a general before a massive battle. During Jesus' final words, He made three huge promises to His disciples. So let's dig deeper to understand His plan for the new Kingdom. These promises were coming soon, but not until *after* Jesus left them. Jesus had already assured them, "It is *better* for you that I go." Here's why:

Promise #1: Power

Jesus was leaving them, but He was not leaving them *alone.* He promised them that they would receive power from the Holy Spirit that would *enable* them to carry out His mission. His mission for them would not depend on their abilities, but rather on the strength given to them by the Holy Spirit. God's mission for the Church in the world is bigger than anything the disciples (or anyone else) can handle on their own. He made this promise because they absolutely needed it. The Holy Spirit will guide them into all truth, remind them of what Jesus said, and convict the world of sin. Power was needed. Power was promised. Power was on the way.

Promise #2: Presence

In another account of Jesus' last words to the disciples, He told them, "I will be with you until the end of the age." (Matthew 28:20) He also said, "I will not leave you desolate; I will come to you." (John 14:18) Even though Our Lord was going to be taken out of their sight, the disciples would experience the presence of Jesus through the Holy Spirit. The Church teaches that the Holy Spirit "proceeds from the Father and the Son." (Nicene Creed) Whenever we experience one person of the Holy Trinity, in a mystical sense, we experience all three. It's impossible to overstate the importance of Jesus' promise to be with His disciples. He meant the world to them. They spent three years of their life with Him. They would undoubtedly *miss* Jesus. Jesus would miss His friends, too. With this promise, perhaps Jesus was thinking of what *He* would need also.

Promise #3: Return

Before the disciples could catch their breath, the angels told them that Jesus would return in the same way He left. "Why do you stand looking into heaven?" they asked. It's as if they were saying, "You guys better get to work because He's coming back!" I love that. Jesus' promise to return comes with an assurance that He will "come to judge the living and the dead" and bring us to the place He has prepared for us in heaven. (Nicene Creed) They had to get busy because Jesus wasn't going to stay away forever.

The spiritual fruit of the Mystery of the Ascension is Hope. We have hope because we know that with the Holy Spirit we can accomplish God's mission. We have hope because Jesus is coming back and we know that He is preparing an incredible place for us. We have hope because we know that Jesus will return to correct this world's wrongs. We have hope because He's coming to get us. The Book of Revelation tells us God will "wipe away every tear from their eyes." (21:4) What an incredible promise!

Where else can humanity find hope like this? Not in politicians or human achievement. Our hope isn't found within ourselves. Our hope will never come from new-age philosophy, self-help fads, or social media influencers. Our hope is found in God alone.

What does it look like for you to live with hope? Have you allowed discouragement to control your life? Hopelessness sometimes happens without us even realizing it. We must not look at the world through the lens of the evil around us or become discouraged by our own shortcomings. Instead, we should see God's plan for the world and trust His promise to work through us. Just like with a motorcycle, our souls will follow where we look, so keep your eyes on Jesus.

Remember, His promises are just as potent today as they were two thousand years ago. When you need the presence of Jesus, go to Him in the tabernacle. When you need His power, call upon the Holy Spirit in prayer. And never forget, whatever is wrong in your world, Jesus is coming back to fix it. Now get to work.

THE DESCENT OF THE HOLY GHOST
Spiritual Fruit—The Gifts of the Holy Spirit

When the day of Pentecost had come, they were all together in one place. And suddenly a sound came from heaven like the rush of a mighty wind, and it filled all the house where they were sitting. And there appeared to them tongues as of fire, distributed and resting on each one of them. And they were all filled with the Holy Spirit and began to speak in other tongues, as the Spirit gave them utterance.

(Acts 2:1-4)

After the Ascension, the disciples and Mary gathered together, waiting to see what would come next. Before He left, Jesus told them to return to Jerusalem and wait for the promise of the Holy Spirit. They had no idea what would happen. No one told them, "This is Acts 2, and it's gonna be awesome!"

Jesus had given them the next step, but that was it. However, He had previously linked baptism to what was coming soon: "for John baptized with water, but before many days you shall be baptized with the Holy Spirit." (Acts 1:5) The disciples waited and prayed.

Then it happened.

The Holy Spirit descended upon them as tongues of fire on their heads. They began to speak the truth of the gospel in languages they didn't know. This is significant because people from many nations had gathered in Jerusalem for the Jewish Feast of Pentecost. They heard the gospel proclaimed in their own languages!

Peter stood up before the huge crowd and boldly proclaimed the good news. "Repent and be baptized!" (Acts 2:38) Three thousand people did just that.

This was the fulfillment of Jesus' promise that the disciples would be His witnesses beginning in Jerusalem, but it didn't stop there. God's mission is to take the gospel of Jesus Christ into the entire world through the ministry of the Church, and it started right there in the Upper Room. The Holy Spirit did not tell them what to say. The Holy Spirit spoke *through* them. That's the glory of God in action!

None of us would be Christians if the events in the Third Glorious Mystery hadn't happened. When we meditate on this mystery, we need to realize that *we* are a part of this story that will never end until the promise of Jesus' triumphant return is fulfilled. The work of the apostles continues in his Church right now.

The spiritual fruit of this mystery is The Gifts of the Holy Spirit. The New Testament mentions gifts of the Holy Spirit in several different places. (Romans 12:6-8; 1 Corinthians 12:8-10; Ephesians 4:11; 1 Peter 4:10-11) These references are not an exhaustive list, but rather serve as examples of what the Holy Spirit can do in the lives of believers.

The Catholic Church traditionally lists seven Gifts of the Holy Spirit, which are derived from the Old Testament book of Isaiah (11:2-3). These gifts are wisdom, understanding, counsel, fortitude, knowledge, piety, and fear of the Lord.

One important aspect of what we see at Pentecost is that the Holy Spirit's power is given not only for the benefit of believers, but also for the benefit of *unbelievers*. The Spirit enabled the apostles to preach to those who didn't know the gospel. There certainly are benefits for those who receive the Gifts because we grow in holiness and the knowledge of God through the Holy Spirit. Yet we must always remember that God's plan for the Church is to bring Christ to the world. When the sun rose on Pentecost, those people in Jerusalem were unbelievers. When the sun went down that night, three thousand believed.

It's easy to get this wrong. It's easy to fall into the trap of treating the Holy Spirit like some sort of magic that gives you a better life or a more exciting faith. I have spent plenty of time in worship gatherings that were focused on the outward "Gifts of the Spirit," but had nothing to do with preaching the gospel.

I remember attending a youth service where people could *take lessons* on how to speak in tongues. I was shocked—I didn't think you could do that. At another service, if people didn't have some sort of visible and dramatic display such as being "slain in the Spirit," the whole group was disappointed. There was often pressure put on people to create these experiences because they seemed to think it gave meaning to their faith. In reality, I think some people just crave excitement and want to see God's glory on display. There's nothing wrong with wanting to see God's glory, but if you really want to see the Holy Spirit in action, get on board with God's mission through His Church.

In Catholicism, the Sacrament of Confirmation is connected to the Gifts of the Holy Spirit. In this sacrament, we willingly cooperate with the grace given to us in Baptism. Here's how the Catechism of the Catholic Church describes it:

> *Baptism, the Eucharist, and the sacrament of Confirmation together constitute the "sacraments of Christian initiation," whose unity must be safeguarded. It must be explained to the faithful that the reception of the sacrament of Confirmation is necessary for the completion of baptismal grace. For "by the sacrament of Confirmation, [the baptized] are more perfectly bound to the Church and are enriched with a special strength of the Holy Spirit. Hence they are, as true witnesses of Christ, more strictly obliged to spread and defend the faith by word and deed.* (CCC 1285)

Spreading the faith "by word and deed" is the key. The Gifts of the Holy Spirit are given to the Church to empower its members to fulfill God's mission. One pastor I know sums it up this way, "The steam is in the engine to move the train, not just to blow the whistle."

As you meditate on this mystery, consider what your life would look like if you were available to God for His plan, no matter what. Consider what it would look like if you placed no limits on what God has planned for others through you.

In the Third Glorious Mystery, the apostles were empowered by God. They did not do it on their own. They were simply the vessels. When we submit ourselves to God by cooperating with the Holy Spirit, we must remember that it's not about us and what we can do for God. God isn't looking for people to do things for Him. God is looking for people He can do things *through*. That's a big difference. That's what this mystery is all about.

The Fourth Glorious Mystery

THE ASSUMPTION OF THE VIRGIN MARY
Spiritual Fruit—The Desire for Heaven

"Finally the Immaculate Virgin, preserved free from all stain of original sin, when the course of her earthly life was finished, was taken up body and soul into heavenly glory, and exalted by the Lord as Queen over all things, so that she might be the more fully conformed to her Son, the Lord of lords and conqueror of sin and death." The Assumption of the Blessed Virgin is a singular participation in her Son's Resurrection and an anticipation of the resurrection of other Christians: In giving birth you kept your virginity; in your Dormition you did not leave the world, O Mother of God, but were joined to the source of Life. You conceived the living God and, by your prayers, will deliver our souls from death.

(CCC 966)

The Assumption of the Virgin Mary reveals the glory of God in a spectacular way. Some would argue with this by saying, "Why all the focus on Mary? Doesn't this take attention away from God?" I used to think this way. Before I entered the Church, I wondered why Catholics made such a big fuss about Mary. After my conversion, I started praying the Rosary and experienced the glory of God in a new way. What I discovered is that His glory is revealed in His handiwork. I love how Pope Benedict XVI puts it:

> *"The Virgin Mary, among all creatures, is a masterpiece of the Most Holy Trinity. In her humble heart full of faith, God prepared a worthy dwelling place for himself to bring to completion the mystery of salvation..."*

> (ANGELUS- Saint Peter's Square,
> Solemnity of the Most Holy Trinity Sunday; June 11, 2006)

God's glory is revealed in His creation in the same way an artist's talent is revealed in his artwork. The Virgin Mary was created by the Father for the specific purpose of being the living, breathing vessel who would carry His Son. In the Old Testament, the Ark of the Covenant contained "the presence" of God. In the New Testament, St. Luke shows us something incredible about Mary. He compares the Old Testament account of King David bringing the Ark to Jerusalem with Mary, pregnant with Jesus, going to visit Elizabeth. (2 Samuel 6; Luke 1:39-45) Mary contained the presence of God in her flesh. This is why the Church Fathers called Our Lady the *New* Ark of the Covenant.

God's plan for Mary is all about motherhood. He desired a pure vessel to carry His Son. In the first Joyful Mystery, we meditated on Mary being "full of grace" at the *beginning* of her life. The Assumption of Mary is a picture of the Mother of God, full of grace, at the *end* of her life. She never stopped being full of grace, so Jesus took her up to heaven to bring her to the place He had prepared for her.

Can you imagine what that place must be like?

> *"In my Father's house are many rooms; if it were not so, would I have told you that I go to prepare a place for you? And when I go and prepare a place for you, I will come again and will take you to myself, that where I am you may be also."*
>
> (John 14:2-3)

We've all seen those videos of soldiers returning from deployment to surprise their loved ones. The soldiers usually stay hidden until the last possible moment before they are revealed to their unsuspecting relatives. When the beautiful reunion happens, well, I don't care who you are, it always brings a tear to your eye. Family reunions are powerful.

My wife Estelle and I know something about this. When our son Drew was deployed to Qatar for a year, one of the ways we consoled ourselves was to make sure that his bedroom was ready for his return. We dusted and vacuumed. We made sure his things were in order. It was pristine and squared away.

Sometimes I would go into his room and just sit there. Being in his personal space made me feel close and connected to him. Preparing his room brought the reality of his future arrival into our present-day experience.

When Drew finally returned home, it was the reunion of a lifetime. We hugged him like never before. Our joy just could not be contained. And then, when he entered his room, you could see the joy and relief on his face. He had been gone for so long, and now he was back with his loved ones in a place that was prepared just for him. Our family was reunited. The universe just felt complete again. I even have a photo of him sitting on his bed, taking off his army boots. There is so much meaning in that moment.

Now let's think of the Assumption of Mary as a family reunion. What was going on in Jesus' heart as He prepared a place for Mary? He made this place glorious just for her. I bet St. Joseph helped Him get it ready. It had to be awesome.

The place Jesus prepared was ready. At the end of Mary's life, He went to get her. Imagining the embrace of the Holy Family in heaven brings tears to my eyes.

My friends, let's take a few moments to reflect on the journey we've taken with Jesus and Mary. The Joyful, Luminous, Sorrowful, and into the Glorious Mysteries—all the images, emotions, people, events, pain, and glorious truths—it's so much to contemplate, which is why the Rosary is such a gift. The Rosary allows us to do what seems impossible—to unite ourselves with Jesus, Mary, the disciples, and all the other people we've met along the way.

All these things and more were in the hearts of Jesus and Joseph when they welcomed Mary to the family reunion, in the place He had prepared for her in heaven. Their embrace encompassed and contained all of it. After everything the Holy Family had been through, it all came full circle at the Assumption.

The spiritual fruit of this mystery is The Desire for Heaven. Mary's love for her Son was the most powerful force in her life. There was never a moment when she chose anything over Him. She didn't feel inconvenienced by God's plan. She never had any ambition other than to do God's will. She never put herself first. She always desired Jesus. She always desired heaven.

Jesus promises those who follow Him that their desire for holiness will be rewarded: "Blessed are those who hunger and thirst for righteousness, for they shall be satisfied". (Matthew 5:6)

Our level of satisfaction will be directly related to our level of desire. As we meditate on this mystery, we must ask ourselves, "What is my strongest desire?" The world does everything it can to foster our desire for things contrary to righteousness. Advertisers know how to make us feel incomplete without whatever they want to sell us. The world tells us to put ourselves first. Self-denial is never viewed as a good thing.

How do we know what we desire most? We start by looking at our behavior. Desire dictates behavior. We all experience this. Sometimes, what we know we *should* want are not the things we *actually* want. Anyone who has ever wrestled with addiction or tried to lose a few pounds understands that what we desire in the moment is often contrary to what is best for us.

When our desire for what is right and good is strongest, we can resist temptation, but when our desire to gratify our flesh is stronger, we rationalize, make excuses, and give in to temptation. This is tough stuff. Who has enough willpower to resist the desires of the flesh?

Fortunately, turning our desires over to God is not about willpower. This is why the greatest commandment is about love, not willpower. Whatever we *love* the most will direct whatever we desire the most, which directs our behavior. When you love yourself more than Jesus, you will desire things that gratify you, which will lead to sin. When you love Jesus more than yourself, you will desire whatever serves and pleases Him, which will lead to righteous behavior.

The Virgin Mary was assumed into heaven and received such a great reward because her love for Jesus was always her strongest desire. The key to controlling your desire is to love Jesus more. When your love for Jesus surpasses your love of self, you will experience a dramatic increase in holiness. As you meditate on this mystery, ask God, through the intercession of the Blessed Virgin Mary, to help you love Jesus more and more. She's the expert.

Each of us will have our own reunion with Jesus one day. After we have completed our earthly life, we will stand before Him. If we have died in friendship with God, we will be taken to the place He has prepared for us in heaven. What a glorious day that will be! Can you think of anything more desirable? Me neither.

THE CORONATION OF THE BLESSED VIRGIN MARY AS QUEEN OF HEAVEN AND EARTH

Spiritual Fruit—The Grace of Final Perseverance

*And a great portent appeared in heaven, a woman
clothed with the sun, with the moon under her feet,
and on her head a crown of twelve stars.*

(Revelation 12:1)

Mary's role as the Mother of God didn't end after Jesus' Death, Resurrection, and Ascension. At the foot of the Cross, Jesus gives her to the Church as "Mother." (John 19:27) Why does the Church need a mother?

The people of God are often described using the imagery of a family. God is our Father. Jesus is the firstborn son. Jesus referred to anyone who does the will of His Father as His "brother, sister, and mother." (Matthew 12:50) We are a family. Our family has a mother—Mary.

Family is God's design and God's plan. After the Ascension of Jesus, Mary remained with the apostles for many years to assist and care for them, and for the Church as it grew.

Her motherhood for the young Church was a great blessing to all. Did it end after her time on earth was finished? Not a chance! When the apostle John sees that incredible vision in Revelation, he sees God's continuing plan for the Blessed Virgin Mary. The scene reminds me of the Transfiguration of Jesus in that a greater vision of God's glory was revealed.

The Coronation of Mary shows us that God's plan for her motherhood *increased* after her Assumption. She has a new role as "Queen Mother of the New Covenant." To understand this mystery, we must look to the role of the Queen Mother of the Old Covenant. In 1 Kings 2, we learn that the queen of the kingdom was not the king's *wife*, but rather his *mother*. For example, King Solomon's mother was Bathsheba. The role of the Queen Mother was to approach her son with the petitions of the people. (2 Kings 10:13) Listen to how the king responds to his mother:

> *So Bathshe'ba went to King Solomon, to speak to him on behalf of Adoni'jah. And the king rose to meet her, and bowed down to her; then he sat on his throne, and had a seat brought for the king's mother; and she sat on his right.*
>
> *Then she said, "I have one small request to make of you; do not refuse me."*
>
> *And the king said to her, "Make your request, my mother; for I will not refuse you.*　　　　　　　　(1 Kings 2:19-20)

In the fifth Glorious Mystery, we see an incredible parallel. In Revelation, John sees the Woman wearing a crown. She is a queen. Who crowned her? Her Son, King Jesus. It's mystical imagery but speaks to a profound reality.

Mary is the new Queen Mother. What a gift to us! Her queenship is about intercession and grace. As our mother, she comforts and nurtures us in the faith. As the queen, she approaches the King on our behalf, *who will not refuse her.* Queen Mother Mary brings grace to us that we might know, love, and serve her Son, King Jesus.

The spiritual fruit of this mystery is The Grace of Final Perseverance. We all know what it's like to begin something and not finish it. How many household projects get started with vision and excitement only to be abandoned when frustration and difficulty arise? How many New Year's resolutions have failed before March 1st (or January 2nd)? How often have we felt motivated to improve, but then failed to sustain that motivation? It happens all the time.

The most tragic situation is when we fail to persevere in our faith. Many people struggle with the need for perseverance in the faith because they mistakenly believe that being a Christian should make life easier. Perseverance, by definition, means that difficult situations are inevitable. If we buy into the false advertising that Christianity doesn't include hardship, we will fall apart when the trouble comes. If we don't expect trials, we won't be prepared for them. The first step towards having perseverance is knowing we need it.

This shouldn't shock anyone who has read even a little of the Bible. God's people have always needed to persevere because this world is full of evil. The Christian life calls us to fight sin, corruption, and oppression. This won't be easy. St. Peter gave us this admonition:

> *Beloved, do not be surprised at the fiery ordeal which comes upon you to prove you, as though something strange were happening to you. But rejoice in so far as you share Christ's sufferings, that you may also rejoice and be glad when his glory is revealed.* (1 Peter 4:12-13)

When we expect that trials are coming, we can stand firm, prepared, and ready for whatever happens. Perseverance isn't only about enduring difficult situations in misery and discouragement. We are called to have joy even amidst these difficulties. St. James tells us,

> *Count it all joy, my brethren, when you meet various trials, for you know that the testing of your faith produces steadfastness. And let steadfastness have its full effect, that you may be perfect and complete, lacking in nothing.* (James 1:2-4)

I love that St. James tells us that the full effect of perseverance is perfection. This is why this is the fruit of the Fifth Glorious Mystery. Our Lady was perfect and steadfast in her life because she was "full of grace." She is the channel of grace to the world because Jesus came through her. As the Queen Mother of Heaven and Earth, she continues to bring Christ to the world and the world to Christ. The grace given to Mary was not just about giving birth to Jesus, but so much more. She never stopped doing the will of God. She never stopped persevering.

What is your understanding of perseverance? Do you believe it's about your own strength? Or do you think you don't have to do anything because God will just take care of everything for you? We must realize that the ability to persevere is the result of grace. We can't do it on our own.

God didn't choose Mary because she was perfect and holy. God created her that way by His grace. She only needed to cooperate with that grace for it to be fulfilled in her life. You and I must also cooperate with grace. God's grace is poured out to us in the sacraments so that we can know, love, and serve Him, but we must always cooperate with it. If we do, we will persevere. If we don't, we will fail.

Cooperating with the Grace of Final Perseverance means receiving grace in the sacraments as often as possible. Frequent confession, communion, fasting, almsgiving, and prayer will help tremendously. Additionally, asking for the intercession of the Queen Mother will do more for you than you could ever do for yourself. The closer you get to Mary, the closer you get to Jesus. If you want to persevere, stay close to the one who brings you the grace you need.

Closing Thoughts

on The Glorious Mysteries

God wins! The glory of God shines brightly through the darkness of the world when we pray the Glorious Mysteries. We need to be people of glory. People of hope. People of anticipation. Meditating on The Glorious Mysteries helps put us in the proper mindset because they celebrate God's victories. These become our victories when we unite ourselves with them in the Rosary. Each time you pray through the Glorious Mysteries, allow the Holy Spirit to set aside the places in your life where you feel defeated, discouraged, and hopeless. God does not want you to live as people who have no hope, but rather as the most hopeful people the world has ever seen.

So we do not lose heart. Though our outer nature is wasting away, our inner nature is being renewed every day. For this slight momentary affliction is preparing for us an eternal weight of glory beyond all comparison, because we look not to the things that are seen but to the things that are unseen;

for the things that are seen are transient, but the things that are unseen are eternal. (2 Corinthians 4:16-18)

May you be renewed every day by the hope you have in Christ. May you feel the weight of the glory of God in your life. And may you always remember the eternal and unseen things which will sustain and bring you joy.

EPILOGUE

As soon as you finish this book, it may be time to start reading it again. The mysteries will continue to offer new insights and challenges every time you pray the Rosary. It isn't a one-and-done prayer. That's a good thing. We need God to speak to us every day. We need to speak to Him every day too. My sincere hope is that this little book helps you to enter into the mysteries of the Rosary each time you pray. So I want to leave you with a two-part challenge.

1. Pray the Rosary every day.

I'm not one for arbitrary rules, but in my experience, praying the Rosary every day has been one of the most transformative things I have ever done. There are so many things you can do to grow in your faith, but give it a try and see what happens. I am confident that your faith will grow in significant ways. Be intentional. Set an appointment. Don't just let it happen—*make* it happen.

2. Keep track of what God is saying to you as you meditate on the mysteries.

Sometimes in life, we hear something profound and think to ourselves, *I need to remember that!* When this happens during prayer, we need to keep track of what God is "telling us." Use a journal or make a recording on your phone—whatever works. When the Holy Spirit gives you an insight, or you experience an answer to prayer, don't let it pass you by. Keeping a record can help you look back on your experiences and lessons learned. Over time, you will learn and grow in your relationship with God as well as your knowledge of the faith. As our lives progress, God shows us new things. That's the fun part of the relationship. Don't miss it!

One more thing—prayerfully consider inviting others to pray the Rosary. It can be with you in person or online. Or maybe you will inspire people to pray on their own. Don't get hung up on the details. Let God worry about that.

You may wonder, what is the best way to share your love of the Rosary with others? It's not rocket science. Live out the spiritual fruits of the Rosary and people will respond. It's often been said, *You can't give away what you don't have.* When you pray the Rosary and meditate on these mysteries, the results will be apparent to others. Let them see in you the beauty of what happens through this incredible prayer.

Finally, people often ask me, "Hey Keith, what is your favorite mystery?"

I have struggled to give a consistent answer. My favorite mystery often changes depending on what's going on in my life. When I am in a trial, I may relate more to the Sorrowful Mysteries so that I can unite my suffering with Jesus. When dealing with self-doubt or fear, I find the Luminous Mysteries especially meaningful. Sometimes the Joyful Mysteries catch me off guard, and like that time in my office preparing a sermon all those years ago, I get choked up when I get to the Annunciation. When it comes to the Glorious Mysteries—the Assumption of Mary reminds me of the reunion I hope to have with my own mother in heaven someday.

I've come to terms with not having a "go-to" favorite mystery. The fact is, they are *all* my favorite. I hope and pray this becomes your experience as well.

Pray the Rosary, my friends.

Enter into the mysteries, and you will find that the mysteries will enter into you.

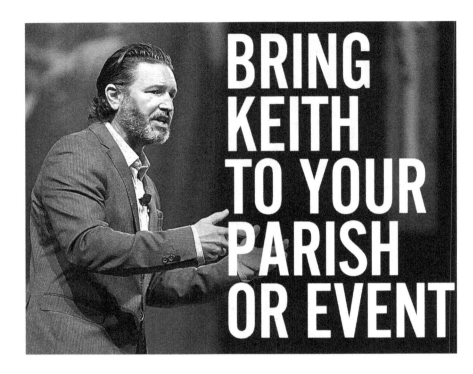

Keith is a dynamic and engaging speaker with followers across the world. He can bring messages on many topics relating to Faith, Conversion to Catholicism, Discipleship and much more. Contact us to discuss your event and check availability.

DOWN ✝o EAR✝H
KEITH NESTER

Bring Keith to your parish or event, visit:
down2earthministry.org

ROSARY CREW

Pray with Keith and thousands of others from all across the world. Go to: youtube.com/rosarycrewwithkeithnester
Make sure to subscribe.

Keith's monthly podcast/video series where he connects the eternal truths of the Catholic faith to everyday life. Subscribe today wherever you find your podcasts and on Youtube. Go to: youtube.com/keithnester
Make sure to subscribe.

UNPACKING THE MASS

Each week, Keith takes listeners through the upcoming readings to open hearts to what God is saying. Subscribe today wherever you find your podcasts and on Youtube. Go to: youtube.com/keithnester
Make sure to subscribe.

To see more of Keith's content, and for more information, visit :

down2earthministry.org

Made in United States
North Haven, CT
07 March 2024

49643604R00088